Embodying Feminist Liberation Theologies

A Special Edition of Feminist Theology

Aims and Objectives of the Journal

The journal *Feminist Theology* aims to engage a wide readership of women and men, of all ages and walks of life, who seek to discover and share in Feminist Theology in all its various forms. The editors start from the understanding that Feminist Theology is a theology of liberation

- to provide a space for women to discuss religion and spirituality
- to empower women who feel marginalized within their religious tradition
- to provide a forum for lively academic exchange
- to include poetry, liturgy, reflective and experiential writing
- to encourage writers and artists in these areas to value their work and to contribute
- to name and challenge those things which are oppressive to women
- to engage the establishment in debate.

The editors intend *Feminist Theology* to reflect its founding principles of experience, mutuality, creativity, respect, joy, nurture, accessible scholarship and 'hearing women to speech'.

FEMINIST THEOLOGY

THE JOURNAL OF THE BRITAIN AND IRELAND
SCHOOL OF FEMINIST THEOLOGY

www.continuumjournals.com

Editorial Committee
Lisa Isherwood, Janet Wootton, Julie Clague, Lillalou Hughes

The views and opinions expressed in *Feminist Theology* are those of their authors and do not necessarily reflect the views of the editorial committee except where otherwise stated.

Feminist Theology is published three times a year, in January, May and September. Please write to The Editorial Committee, 72 Norbury Crescent, London SW16 4IA, regarding submitting material to the editors.

Continuum Publishing Ltd
The Tower Building, 11 York Road, London SE1 7NX and
15 East 26th Street, Suite 1703, New York, NY 10010, USA

Information for Subscribers: For information about Continuum books, please log on to www.continuumbooks.com
For information about Continuum journals, please log on to www.continuumjournals.com

SUBSCRIPTION
Subscription prices (prices include second-class postal delivery within the UK and air-mail delivery elsewhere):

	UK/Europe/Rest of the World	The Americas
Individuals	£30.00	$47.50
Institutions	£60.00	$95.00

Canadian customers/residents please add 7% for GST onto the Americas price.

Postmaster: Send address changes to Orca Book Services, Stanley House, 3 Fleets Lane, Poole, Dorset BH15 3AJ.
Sample Requests, New Orders, Renewals, Claims/Other Subscription Matters: Contact the Journals Subscription Administrator, Orca Journals, Stanley House, 3 Fleets Lane, Poole, Dorset BH15 3AJ (tel: +44 [0]1202 785 712; fax: +44 [0]1202 666 219); or journals@orcabookservices.co.uk (cheques should be made payable to Orca Journals; claims for missing issues must be made no later than three months after publication).
Advertising: For details contact jrnladvert@continuumbooks.com or the Journals Advertising Manager, Continuum, The Tower Building, 11 York Road, London SE1 7NX.
Microform: This journal is available in microform from the Serials Acquisitions Department, Bell & Howell Information and Learning, 300 North Zeeb Road, Ann Arbor, MI 48106, USA.
Back Issues: Available from Orca Journals, Stanley House, 3 Fleets Lane, Poole, BH15 3AJ. Prices upon request.

Copyright: All rights reserved. Apart from fair dealing for the purposes of research or private study, or criticism or review, as permitted under the UK Copyright, Designs and Patents Act 1988, no part of this publication may be reproduced, stored or transmitted by any means without the prior written permission of the Publisher, or in accordance with the terms of photocopying licenses issued by the organisations authorised by the Publisher to administer reprographic reproduction rights. Authorisation to photocopy items for educational classroom use is granted by the Publisher provided the appropriate fee is paid directly to the Copyright Clearance Center, 222 Rosewood Drive, Danvers, MA 01923, USA from whom clearance should be obtained in advance.

Indexing and Abstracting: This journal is indexed in the *ATLA Religion Database*, published by the American Theological Library Association, 250 S. Wacker Dr., 16th Flr, Chicago, IL 60606, USA (email: atla@atla.com, WWW: www.atla.com), *ZellerDietrich Bibliographische Verlage*, Zeitschrifteneingang, Hirschberger Strasse 17B, D-49086 Osnabrück, Germany (email: zeller@zeller.os.uunet.de, WWW: www.dietrich-bibliogr.de), it is abstracted in Religious and Theological Abstracts, PO Box 215, Myerstown, PA 17067, USA (email: rtabst@leba.net, WWW: www.rtabst.org) and it is also indexed and abstracted in the *Religion & Philosophy Collection* and *Academic Search Premier* published by EBSCO Publishing, 10 Estes St., PO Box 682, Ipswich, MA 01938, USA (email: ep@epnet.com, WWW: www.epnet.com).

© The Continuum Publishing Group Ltd 2004
ISSN 0966-7350
ISBN 0-56708-421-3
Printed and bound by MPG Books Ltd, Bodmin, Cornwall

Contents

Introduction
Beverley Clack — 133-135

The Liturgy
Agnes Rafferty — 136-139

The Embodiment of Feminist Liberation Theology: The Spiralling of Incarnation
Lisa Isherwood — 140-156

'Pussy, Queen of Pirates': Acker, Isherwood and the Debate on the Body in Feminist Theology
Marcella Althaus-Reid — 157-167

A Theology of Corporeality Embodied in the Butch Femme Bar Culture of the 1950s and 1960s
Marie Cartier — 168-186

Politics of Sexuality
Pauline [Asphodel] Long — 187-202

Witches and Words
Naomi R. Goldenberg — 203-211

Theaological Reflections on Embodiment
Ruth Mantin — 212-227

Exploding Mystery: Feminist Theology and the Sacramental
Elizabeth Stuart — 228-236

Sex and Death: Spirituality and Human Existence
    Beverley Clack   237-252

With Critical Voices
    Angie Pears   253-260

Introduction

Beverley Clack

This collection of essays arose from the papers given at a one-day conference to mark the celebrations that greeted Lisa Isherwood's appointment as Professor of Feminist Liberation Theologies at the College of St Mark and St John, Plymouth, in May 2002. The professorship came as timely recognition of Lisa's important work in the area of Feminist Theology, and should be a cause for celebration for all women working in this area. The 'glass ceiling' may still exist, but here is another exemplar whose experience suggests that it is not completely unbreakable. A founder member of the Britain and Ireland School of Feminist Theology, and an editor of the journal *Feminist Theology*, Lisa's career to date has been marked by a desire to further the aims of the women's movement, and, in particular, to support women engaged in the task of theology. As editor of the *Introductions in Feminist Theology* series co-published by Sheffield Academic Press and Pilgrim Press, she has furthered these ends, as the series aims to make feminist theology accessible to women within and outside the academy. Those of us fortunate enough to know Lisa personally will testify to the warmth of her personality, and the very real encouragement that she offers those engaged in feminist theologising. Lisa makes one feel that 'sisterhood' is far from an empty word, and it is with typical generosity of spirit that she sees this Chair as recognition not just of her own work, but the work of all feminist theologians.

It would, however, be a peculiar introduction that failed to say something about the significance of Lisa's work for the field of feminist theology. Her work is defined by the clarity of its expression, and her *Introducing Feminist Theology*,[1] written with Dorothea McEwan, has rightly taken on the status of a classic text, introducing countless students to the issues and methods of feminist theologising. More recently, her *Liberating Christ* (1999)[2] addresses in characteristically robust terms the

---

1. Lisa Isherwood, *Introducing Feminist Theology* (Sheffield: Sheffield Academic Press, 1993).
2. Lisa Isherwood, *Liberating Christ* (Cleveland, OH: Pilgrim Press, 1999).

need to liberate Christianity from its historical use as a tool of oppression, in order that it might become, in the words Rosemary Radford Ruether uses in her Foreword to this work, a 'vehicle of redemptive life' (p. vii). Lisa rejects the dualism of Greek metaphysics and its accompanying imperialistic power, which has distorted the potentially liberating message of Christianity. She ends this work with a typically passionate rallying cry for a Christianity which does not neglect the body, but which is grounded in it: 'Seize your moment—enflesh the Christ you profess to believe in'.[3]

The title that Lisa chose for her Chair is significant, and each of the terms within it says much about her understanding of what it means to be a feminist theologian. She is Professor of *Feminist* Liberation Theologies. In a climate where it is not an easy thing to call oneself 'feminist', when we supposedly live in a 'post'-feminist age, when there is pressure for a more 'inclusive' approach to 'gender' studies, the deliberate choice of this word says much about Lisa's continued commitment to the political and spiritual liberation of women. And given recent reports of the injustices women throughout the world still suffer,[4] it seems that claims of feminism's demise are at best overly optimistic ('we don't need feminism any more') and at worst deliberately designed to obfuscate the continuing oppression of women.

And so the fact that Lisa is Professor of Feminist *Liberation* Theologies is also important. Feminism is not, and never can be, simply an intellectual stance. To call oneself 'feminist' is to engage in political and social struggle, and thus 'liberation' should be an important part of what feminism is about. Making the connection between feminist thinking and liberation theology may not be new, but in an age in which an emphasis on theory threatens to dominate much academic feminist writing, thus distancing it from the lived experience of women, it is important that this commitment be expressed once more, and with the kind of passion that Lisa brings to all her work.

This is not to say that the notion of 'feminist theology' is unproblematic: as womanist theologians have pointed out, all too often the concerns of feminist theologians have been the concerns of white, middle class, professional women. And by choosing the title 'Professor of Feminist Liberation *Theologies*' Lisa has drawn attention to the importance of recognising diversity in Feminist Theology. Mainstream theology may be marked by the desire to systematise and unify its writings: feminists

---

3. Isherwood, *Liberating Christ*, p. 150.
4. As I write this, the media is reporting that many numbers of Romanian women are being sold into sexual slavery (Channel 4 News, 11 February 2003).

© The Continuum Publishing Group Ltd 2004.

are perhaps more open to the challenges and opportunities of recognising and celebrating the diverse nature of feminist writing on religion and the divine. Such openness is not a weakness of the field, but perhaps constitutes its strength: as this collection shows. There is agreement, but also disagreement; yet what underpins the very different content of these papers is the desire of the writers to engage with women's lives, issues and experiences, and to use this engagement not only to challenge patriarchal norms, but also their own ideas and assumptions. We have come a long way from an unproblematic use of the term 'women's experience', and the recognition of difference is most important.

And so this collection stands not only as a celebration of the point that we—and Lisa herself—have reached, but also directs us to the future. Feminist theology and studies in religion remain some of the most innovative and consistently self-reflexive and self-critical pieces of work, and the papers presented here suggest some of the new directions that feminist theology/theologies might take. In celebrating Lisa's Chair we are celebrating the opportunity for further collaboration and conversation between us, and we invite readers to join with us in determining the future shape of feminist theology.

© The Continuum Publishing Group Ltd 2004.

The Liturgy

Agnes Rafferty

Procession: Choir,
          Chaplain, Principal, Lisa

Processional Music: *Crossing the Lines for Justice*

Welcome from Revd Cate Edmonds, Chaplain
Welcome from Dr John Rea, Principal

ALL: Lisa we welcome you
And we welcome one another
As we affirm the divine source of all living and loving.
The reality that lies between us and enfolds us, the dynamic spring of our risk taking,
our lovemaking and our celebration of justice.

MC: Today is a day of rejoicing and celebration here at the College of St Mark and St John. It is the day on which this Christian community honours the dignity of women by inaugurating Europe's first Professor of Feminist Liberation Theology. And in so doing offers a challenge to those worldwide in church and community who still refuse, through doctrines of exclusion and unjust laws, to accept the full humanity of women.

We stand here, gathered from our very diverse lives, to witness to the image of the divine in the lives of women. To witness to those who have used their power and gifts in the service of women's dignity and liberation and to call forth, in our generation and the next, the empowerment of women, the liberation of men and the gentle embrace of the planet. And so we passionately proclaim the divine as our birthright and we boldly affirm our identity and our common hope as we celebrate together this community's acknowledgment of women.

Music: *Sophia's Chant*

MC: We are mindful of the times when we have feared to dance for freedom or have rested in the comfort of conformity and refused to engage with our imagination and passion to find new ways and liberating spaces. It is easy to forget how far we still have to go in our struggles for justice and our journeys of liberation. However, we are not alone and other women have kept the vision alive and the struggles moving on — they have been our inspiration as we are the inspiration for others in the spiral of sisterhood.

Music: *I Remember the Women*

We remember women, often forgotten, named and unnamed, who have believed in the power of the divine in their living and loving. Women who have dared to reach out to others; who have dared to dream and to make their dreams, visions and their visions, reality.

Blessed be their honoured names — some of which we now speak.

You may wish to light a candle in honour of a woman, living or dead, known to you personally or through your tradition, who has inspired you. You may simply just wish to speak a name.

MC: We have strong, passionate, vital companions on our journeying. We are empowered by those many generous and gifted women who have touched our lives.

ALL: Retaining their integrity
Making/breaking bread
Taking risks for justice
Giving their lives
Giving life to others
Standing firm
Daring to fear
Daring to love
Daring to claim their divine empowerment.

© The Continuum Publishing Group Ltd 2004.

MC: The following is a creed prepared by Latin American women for the Bejiing Conference in 1994. For Feminist Liberation Theologians it is not a statement of orthodoxy but rather a manifesto of praxis — of making and making again in the face of all unmaking.

ALL: Bread

A clean sky

Active peace

A woman's voice singing somewhere,
melody drifting like smoke from the
cookfires.

The army disbanded,
the harvest abundant

The wounded healed
the child wanted
the prisoner freed
the body's integrity honoured,
the lover returned.

The labour equal fair and honoured.

Delight in the challenge for consensus to solve
problems.

No hand raised in anything but greeting

Secure interiors of heart, home, land so
firm as to make secure borders
irrelevant at last

And everywhere
Laughter, care, celebration, dancing,
contentment and a humble earthly paradise, in the now.

Music: *Freedom Come*

MC: We commit ourselves to the struggle of passion and pain and the hope we find in and between us, our desire to create together an earthly paradise of liberation and life in abundance.

With this vision before us we offer symbolic gifts to Lisa which not only signify her part in the struggle but also offer to the Chair of Feminist Liberation Theology the visions and aspirations of our community.

Lisa receives 13 symbols of her commitment to Feminist Liberation Theology.

Music: *Dancing Sophia's Circle*

MC: In many different ways Lisa has accompanied us on our journeys, laughing with us, crying with us, challenging but holding us, dreaming with us and encouraging and enabling us to embody our visions. Always pushing boundaries.

We now commit ourselves to work with her as she continues to push boundaries and struggle with humour and tears for the greater dignity and life in abundance of women.

Music: *Go Forth Sister*

ALL: In solidarity with the ground of our being and each other we find strength to continue the dance of liberation, sometimes mournful, sometimes ecstatic — but always passionate.

MC: Sisters and brothers we leave to continue the messy/risky/joyous dance of liberation just as Miriam our foresister did with her brothers, Moses and Aaron, and the whole of their people.

Music: *Wade in the Water.*

The Embodiment of Feminist Liberation Theology: The Spiralling of Incarnation

Lisa Isherwood

I have been asked more than once, what does the title of the lecture mean? Well, inevitably, it means many things some of which I will explore. However, the most obvious meaning is found in all of us here who have been, and are, involved in the many and diverse struggles for women's dignity, equality and humanity. I am moved by seeing in the audience women who have dedicated their lives to expanding the social, political and religious/theological space that we as women and men share: women who have been my inspiration and to whom I owe so much. Thank you sisters for your unshakeable belief in justice and your enduring strength.

Beginning the March of the Women

From the moment Nelle Morton[1] suggested that feminist theology was 'hearing one another to speech' she situated the theology that women do in the body. We hear and we speak, but we do not simply hear the word of God, disembodied and dictatorial, but rather the words of each other, challenging us to right the wrongs, to redeem the relationships between us and embody the divine in our lives. We have for many years now engaged in this expanding, enfleshed hermeneutical spiral; we have spoken, heard and reflected upon the experience of women in the light of our religious traditions. We have begun to hear the bodies of women and to place them as word within our religious and theological reflections; we have cautiously and with much trepidation allowed the flesh to show us the divine rather than submitted to the divine moulding of the flesh. In short we have, through our body knowing and through trusting that knowing, entered a revolution, a passionate revolution; one that speaks as loudly of our engagement and commitment to incarnation as it does to our love and valuing of our bodies. It is a revolution embedded in women's erotic power, which understands the body as both the ongoing, alive critique of oppression and the site of struggles for liberation.

1. Nelle Morton, *The Journey is Home* (Boston: Beacon Press, 1985).

However, before getting too carried away with that strand of thought it may be helpful to explain why we got there. Those of us who come from a Christian tradition have been taught in the bosom of mother church that flesh does not matter, that we can be misled and deceived by it and that as women we are the most fleshy, the most deceptive and the most misleading of all creations. This view has sprung from dualism which is deeply embedded in our tradition, and like Japanese knot weed it is very difficult to find its end and its beginning and almost impossible to root it out, but also like knot weed dualistic thinking strangles any self worth we may dare or any blossoming we may feel compelled to venture. Why? Well, because dualism is a device lurking in the midst of an incarnational religion that has objectified us and made us aliens in our own skin. It has weighed heavy on women, men and the planet since it acts as a deadener, a delayer, a tricky device to make us believe in the sanctity of the absent, the corruption of the present, the promise of tomorrow and the inadequacy/incompleteness of today.

Feminist theologians have not simply taken exception to dualism because we wish to demonstrate that we think differently. Rather we have observed what it does in people's lives and to the planet. That kind of split thinking allows us to distance ourselves, and our God, from all we do not feel comfortable with and to set in place systems that oppress and marginalize 'others'. This way of viewing the world creates a large number of 'others' and allows many perceived ills to be heaped upon them. We are all familiar with the divine hierarchy created by Christian dualistic thinking; God, angels/saints, man, woman, planet and in addition the dualisms of black/white, straight/gay, and so on; the list is endless. As we women began to take seriously our own embodiment we came to realise that this is not simply an abstract thought pattern but one that has profoundly damaging effects in our lives. We observed that this way of thinking devised by men enabled them, with extreme humility, to define and take all the good bits for themselves—rationality not emotionality, spirit not flesh, culture not nature; and Christian history shows very clearly how women's bodies have borne the brunt of this schizophrenic way of thinking. The problem has been that Christian history has been read through dualistic lenses and so our beginnings, rooted in Eden, which should declare to us the story of an adventurous, in-tune and divinely-curious woman gives us instead Eve who in one simple action brought about the downfall of man which resulted in the necessary death of the son of God to make amends. The result is that women have been chained to a history of guilt and shame and a theological framework that excludes and reduces us at every turn—a heavy burden to bear. Our place in the story of salvation is then a less than splendid one;

we have come to represent all that humanity needs to be saved from—flesh and nature. Rosemary Radford Ruether[2] has systematically looked at the legacy that has been bequeathed to women by such thinking but Elisabeth Johnson sums it up when she says:

> the idea that the Word might have become female flesh is not even seriously imaginable, so thoroughly has androcentric Christology done its work of erasing the full dignity of women as christomorphic in the community of disciples...as a logical outcome women's salvation is implicitly put in jeopardy...at least in theory.[3]

Against this background our storytelling about the reality of our lives, our real concerns, our theology and the ensuing questioning led to a somewhat surprising theological point; where we were looking again at the core of our religion, incarnation: a concept that declares the full flourishing/redemption of all, yet when viewed only as fully evident in Christ, laid such a reducing, restricting burden on the lives of women. In our struggle for bodily integrity, in our efforts to hear ourselves—and others, in an attempt to become truly embodied, we have had to challenge the Christ of traditional theology. Many courageous sisters, whose commitment to the lived reality of women formed the bedrock of their scrupulous, scholarly engagement with scripture and tradition, have looked again at this apparent contradiction; courageous because they have risked, and suffered, expulsion from their worship communities and the academy. I wish I could say that this was in the 'old days' but sadly I cannot.

Feminist theologians, from very diverse contexts, have highlighted time and again how this dualistic Christ, and the divided world over which he presides, has damaged women, children and the planet. Our womanist sisters[4] have shown how this bleached Christ, the one who is white and can never be black, has been the stick with which to exploit and marginalize their people. Indeed, it was this constructed Christ who justified the march into slavery, the abuse and dehumanising treatment within it and the reluctance to abolish it. The memories of those inhuman times have made womanists very anxious about notions of surrogate suffering; their family histories show them the falsity of such belief. While Chinese women have shown us the false assumptions that are held by

---

2. Rosemary Radford Ruether, *Women and Redemption* (New York: Routledge).
3. Elisabeth Johnson, *She Who Is: The Mystery of God in Feminist Theological Discourse* (New York: Crossroad, 1992), p. 51.
4. See for example, Kelly Brown Douglas, *The Black Christ* (Maryknoll, NY: Orbis Books, 1994); Jacqueline Grant, *White Woman's Christ, Black Woman's Jesus* (Atlanta: Scholars Press, 1989).

those who divide the world according to oppositional categories, rather than seeing it as correlation, as interdependent and interpenetrating; in other words those who believe in hypostatic union or any other dualistic doctrine. Those who hold to a sexually pure notion of Christ are in for a shock when they hear that women in Mexico understand those of their number who are in sex work to be Christ incarnate – the embodiment of redemptive praxis – offering their bodies for the lives of others, their children and extended families. They may also be caught unaware when they hear that Indian women understand the blood that women shed in abortions, abuse and even menstrual blood to be the real blood of life, not that shed on the cross.

It has become clear that the embodiment of feminist liberation theology cannot be achieved if it is underpinned by the Christ of traditional dualistic thinking. That Christ requires that we give up too much of our selves and distort our feelings in the pursuit of disembodied perfection. The struggle for embodiment is a hard fought one, and simply being alive is not enough because we have been subjected to alienation within our own skin for far too long. In a desperate attempt to claim our embodiment as positive, feminists have to face the hard questions about their traditions, and within the Christian tradition we have to realise that we may have to move on beyond the neatly packaged Christ to a place of uncertainty, a place of new imaginings. We will have to look again with courage and imagination at metaphysics, at the dictation of Word becoming flesh and hijacking wisdom, at risk, and what that really requires, and at power – an issue that feminists have had more ease denouncing than claiming, and we will have to engage with new questions, questions that we never thought possible.

It is true to say that even in non-feminist theology the Christ of imperial absolutes is dying. He is being attacked by post-colonial discourse, liberation theology, post-modernism, post-feminism, post-structuralism – the 'posts' are endless. There is no place any more for the imperial lord who brought death, destruction and slavery in his wake to millions. From many diverse situations it is being highlighted that the Greek Christ is deeply problematic. As a Christian community we have a chance; the world is highlighting how misguided we have been. Can we be courageous enough not to simply entrench in old beliefs but to take the challenge and grasp our own lives as those of the divine amongst us?

Christ without Metaphysics-Queer Indeed!

While feminist theology has been scrupulous in its engagement with dualism it has been rather more reticent in relation to metaphysics; believing,

I think, that dualism is a misguided interpretation of, and not a necessary outcome of, imaging the metaphysical realm as we do. Even when we have not engaged consciously with matters metaphysical the outline of this heritage has scarred our thinking. Why scarred? Because it is a way of thinking that does not and can never allow us to take incarnation as seriously as I think we should. While incarnation remains something that happened to someone else, whose mother was genetically interfered with, and all we have to do is believe, it is my opinion that we do not do justice to the struggles in the life of Jesus and the rich narrative that we have been asked to engage with. Therefore we have to get brutal with metaphysics! Is it because I am a Celt that I wish to downplay metaphysics? When the mists lie low over the mountain tops it is easy to understand that the gap between the human and the divine is ruach, a breath — or one small step into uncertainty. I wish to take incarnation seriously; and this is not possible through the veil of Greek metaphysics, that early fossilising impostor into the narrative of the Jesus movement. My theological project has been, and remains, one of exploring radical incarnation; trying to grasp what it is we may hope to live if we take incarnation in the raw without the comfort of other worlds and delayed parousias. If we dare to believe that the human and the divine dwell in one flesh and that flesh is ours. Christianity has as its guiding foremother, Judaism, a religion that understands the historical process as the divine process; a religion that states time and again how the divine was known and seen walking with the people — Sophia herself rolling up her sleeves and getting involved in the everyday life of the market place. Christianity, it seems to me, declared that the divine totally abandoned herself to flesh, thus truly embedding the divine process in the historical/material moment. It can be argued that this was a moving beyond metaphysics — a statement of total trust in the flesh to save the world.

But what happens to Christology and talk of incarnation if we attempt to take them beyond metaphysics? I have argued that we will come in line with the Jesus movement, and the radical praxis of liberation that spiralled amongst his friends and followers, if we give up the virtual reality rhetoric of metaphysics and simply get real. I am not arguing that we should give up on utopian visions, or that we should even abandon our Christian narrative tradition, only that we should take seriously the story we have told ourselves, which is that God left the heavens in order that the full reality of life in abundance may come to being. In order that we may embody justice seeking, mutual relation and radical risk taking — embody feminist liberation theology.

© The Continuum Publishing Group Ltd 2004.

I am mindful of my dear friend Liz Stuart's warnings about abandoning metaphysics—where else can we find the critical distance and the necessary alternative perspective she asks, if we give up this realm? I stand alongside Mary Daly[5] and Elisabeth Schüssler-Fiorenza[6] when I answer that it is to be found in our fantasies and our utopian visions, both of which find fuel in our narrative heritage. Those who have told the stories before us have always urged our young to dream dreams and our elders to see visions—feminist theology urges them to speak those dreams and to befriend each other in the embodying of the visions.

But can a case be made for a non-metaphysical, or differently metaphysical, liberating vision spurred on by the powerful memory of the man Jesus and his followers? In a real sense the embodiment of feminist liberation theology demands it; but can it be done? I wish to offer a few suggestions for alternative readings of the resources we have.

The stories we have told ourselves are truly fantastic. They stretch our minds and challenge our perceptions even of our own physical reality; they can fuel us and they could, if we really believed them, transform the world. Christianity tells stories of strange, queer transformations, of unstable categories and bodies all enacted through the body of a man who proclaimed 'God with us'. As Graham Ward[7] has pointed out, it is through these many changes from divine to flesh, from flesh and blood to bread and wine and from human into cosmic spirit that Christians suggest the world has been redeemed. We have however contained these engaging stories by believing them only possible if we place a shield of metaphysics and exclusivity around them thus making them stable and clear categories and thereby showing our lack of faith in their transforming power and the power of the body to redeem of which these stories scream. We have not dared to believe the relatively new and challenging stories that we have begun to tell ourselves, and have instead found comfort in the very old stories of hero Gods and how they can, if they choose, save us. Christ becomes an old fashioned redeemer and we can go back to sleep in the comfort of those all-powerful arms. However, this is no innocent sleep, it is a sleep of betrayal, betrayal of our own divine birthright and a selling out of ourselves and the whole of creation: betrayal because as we sleep we give up our power, becoming disempowered and dependent. We need to find ways for our stories to permeate our whole being rather

5. Mary Daly, *Beyond God the Father* (London: Women's Press, 1986).
6. Elisabeth Schüssler-Fiorenza, *Jesus: Miriam's Child, Sophia's Prophet* (Critical Issues in Feminist Christology; New York: Continuum, 1994).
7. Graham Ward, 'The Gendered Body of Jesus', in M. Hayes, W. Porter and D. Tombs (eds.), *Religion and Sexuality* (Sheffield: Sheffield Academic Press, 1998), pp. 170-92.

© The Continuum Publishing Group Ltd 2004.

than remain in our heads, where we can play with them and remove them from our real consciousness or turn them into comfort blankets.

Our narrative heritage is rich and, depending on how we read it, embodied. For example the temptations of Jesus illustrate for me his own rejection of matters to do with the world being worked out in the metaphysical realm: turn stones into bread, fly without wings, acquire power in the world while sacrificing your own to another. These suggestions from the devil were all categorically rejected by Jesus who instead moved amongst the people and engaged with them in struggles for justice and liberation. It seems clear then that right from the beginning what Christians have understood as redemption does not occur through cosmic intervention but through passionate engagement with the world and those in it. Have those who rely too heavily on metaphysics for their theology sold out to the devil?

The resurrection is a great and powerful story, found in many cultures. For many Christians the power of Christ is seen to lie in the resurrection without which they would argue there is no Christianity. It is very tempting to see the resurrection as an event solely connected with the man Jesus. If we do this we reduce its power; it becomes, as has famously been said, a conjuring trick with a bag of bones. And we believe it or we don't; we are not required to embrace it as redemptive praxis in our lives. Those who 'witnessed the resurrection' experienced a powerful memory of a man and his message, that is the power to resist embedded in passionate and intimate connection. It is not insignificant that this memory may have been triggered by the breaking of bread together, an embodied and enfleshed action, one rooted in sensuality. Through living and sharing their lives, and through the power of shared memory and action, a stunned and disheartened group were able to rekindle their passion for continued political engagement. This power is not lost with the person, it lives in praxis and mutual relation. Is it too outrageous to suggest that the stories of transfiguration and ascension signalled the acceptance of the departure of the man but a personal embrace of the erotic power which remains constant? Is that what the tongues of fire at Pentecost really symbolised, the passion and empowerment of accepting one's incarnation through finding a voice? Do we too need to experience a transfiguration or an ascension of our own, letting go and embracing the power that lies in the fibre of our beings?

Embodying Word!

Feminist theologians who engage with bodies celebrate the fact that our stories portray Jesus as a very earthy man sharing touch, engaging with nature, making strong political statements through the symbolic use of food; both during the 'last supper' and in the feedings of thousands Jesus enacted shared power and the interconnected nature of flourishing. The actions, that are now Eucharistic, are powerful political symbols since all receive equally in cultures where inequality of access to food and wealth are blatantly obvious. This man got personal; he used fluid from his body to heal and so truly understood the importance of engaging the body in the struggle for liberation. Heyward[8] has developed the idea of dunamis and erotic connection which she understands to be the raw energy that is our divine birthright and which is truly embraced in open vulnerability and mutuality in relation with others. Is this what our stories are attempting to engage us in; an intimate and transforming revolution through something as simple and as powerfully frightening as touch.

The power of touch has been forgotten. Perhaps this is because the Church Fathers could only focus on its negative power and so laid such strong prohibitions against it. But we need to reconnect with our unfolding history of intimacy and empowerment. Elisabeth Moltmann-Wendell[9] and Rita Brock[10] are just two theologians who have demonstrated that we can transform the world through touch — the former does close biblical work to highlight how the texts changed subtly over the years and excluded the related nature of the power of touch in such stories as the woman with the haemorrhage; while the latter declares us all to be broken-hearted healers who require the power of touch to transform us and therefore the world. Brock also emphasises how the healings that we read about as part of our narrative heritage are political. They are not power exerted over another but empowerment shared, resulting in the person healed having the power to resist those oppressive circumstances that caused the need for healing in the first place. Sickness highlights many of the dysfunctions in our world and the healer takes these on board through both suffering them and opposing them in society, this is not only the domain of the healed. Both women declare that there is something essential about the sensuality and earthiness of the way in which we are told Jesus engaged with bodies — they suggest that this points us towards sensuality being part of our redemptive praxis and therefore something that we should embody. We should be embracing

8. Carter Heyward, *Touching Our Strength: The Erotic as Power and the Love of God* (New York: HarperCollins, 1989).
9. Elisabeth Moltmann-Wendell, *A Land Flowing With Milk and Honey* (London: SCM Press, 1986).
10. Rita Brock, *Journeys By Heart. A Christology of Erotic Power* (New York: Crossroad, 1988).

© The Continuum Publishing Group Ltd 2004.

our own body and the bodies of others, in an empowering dance of liberation, not running from flesh for fear of contamination to seek answers set in stone. Embodiment poses ever-unfolding questions, not answers. Incarnation calls us to deep connection and this, I believe, is best rooted in bodies not metaphysics.

If we look at it this way the Jesus narrative enables the flesh to become word and is not *The Word* made flesh. Feminist liberation theology, by placing experience as the starting point of theological reflection, moves us back to our bodies. The body emerges as a place of revelation and moral imperatives. In this way, then, the flesh is speaking and being heard as a site of positive theological significance.

The flesh made word enables us to find a voice and to make our desires known. There are any number of examples of how this vision transforms the landscape of our lives: those who are starving present themselves not as cases for pity but as moral imperatives for the rest of us, as challenges to redress the imbalances in food distribution; those who are poisoned by toxic waste challenge the ethics of business and profit and call into focus the integrity of the planet as well as people; while those who labour under the genocidal reality of advanced capitalism present their bodies as a moral challenge to find alternative economic systems. When the flesh is word these questions cannot be delayed or avoided; there can be no talk of reward in heaven. The bodies of these people are their heaven or hell; they will not wait and be soothed by pious utterances and promises of tomorrow.

Taking the flesh as word also demands that absolutes be placed to one side and listening take the place of unilateral dictation. Reality is constantly changing and what is required is the liberation of empowered speech and hearing not the misplaced confidence of eternal answers. The flesh has been silenced by metaphysics, hierarchy and, once and for all, incarnation. The flesh made word speaks but not just from the head, through the whole body; and it is this voice that returns power to people. Of course, it comes with no guarantees of perfect or even desirable outcomes. We are forced to face up to the realities of crushing defeats as well as glorious successes; there is no metaphysical realm in which to hide we have to see things as they are.

Embodying Risk

Committing to flesh is a risky business—there are any number of outcomes; metaphysics stacks the deck, incarnation randomly throws us into possibilities. However, risking embodiment is perfectly in line with a religion that has incarnation at the heart. Becoming flesh is risky—the stories of the creation of the world and the crucifixion highlight just how risky — nothing is guaranteed once we commit to life. The freedom from divine dictation required for the truly diverse wonder of creation to be made manifest is a huge risk. God took the risk of leaping into flesh, yet we have been encouraged to resist our enfleshment. In short, we have not dared to risk our own divine incarnation. The embodiment of feminist liberation theology urges us to give up notions of personal salvation and to embrace liberation and those utopian visions we have fossilised in kingdom language; it urges us to take big risks.

Incarnation acknowledged as risk means that the kingdom, our visions, are always on a knife's edge between the gloriously successful empowerment of ourselves and others, the devastatingly wrong and the mundanely unimaginative. If we are to break out of the hold that oppressive systems increasingly seem to have on the world then vision empowered by imagination is crucial. We have to be alive to counter-cultural possibilities, to living transgressively. Indeed, we have to incarnate transgression, that is we have to play with existing categories and break boundaries. By limiting our incarnational understanding to just one man we are in danger of reliving his limitations and prejudices and we see from the stories that he appeared to have some; the woman with the haemorrhage and the Syro-Phoenician woman are just two examples that show that incarnation is not without a context or without need of a helping hand, or a push in the right direction. Living transgressively spurs us on to be limitless and without boundary; it requires that we face imaginatively those erected in our own minds, cultures, religious systems and environments and overcome them through the power of intimate connection.

Embodying Power

The raw, dynamic energy that exists within and between us is the power of incarnation, the power that can burst out and transform. It seems entirely possible that what the early Christian writers were conveying about incarnation was not a once and for all event but the knowledge that unless we are fully in our bodies we will never be able to fully explore our divinity. Even the early Fathers, as influenced as they were by Greek dualism, understood that Jesus was most fully divine when he was most fully human, that Christ became man in order that all may become divine. I would, of course, like to change their emphasis but accept their vision. It was not the incarnation of the only son of God that allowed believers to achieve union with the divine, but the bursting forth of the divine that makes it possible for all of us to grasp the same power 'anyone who makes an opening as he did wants others to enlarge it'.[11] The task then is to bring the power of our incarnation to the forefront, to make empowered living real. Perhaps when we grasp the power of erotic connection between us, we will have collapsed the final barrier to empowerment that dualism sets in place, that is, the uniqueness of Christ.

But we are afraid of power, particularly embodied power. This is no coincidence since Eve is set before us as an example of how afraid we should really be: interacting with the world in a truly sensual and embodied way, taking joy as she did in the beauty of creation results in expulsion from paradise. However, as Mary Daly[12] has pointed out, that may not be too bad since the male has conceived of paradise as a walled-in, confined space where freedom is limited. This is not the ideal surrounding for the embodiment of anything let alone liberation; we need a more expansive and adventurous space in which to flourish, one in which we can explore and learn. Feminist liberation theologians seeking embodiment have burst out of paradise, we have come to see Eve as the foremother of another tradition that encouraged engagement with the real stuff of life in order to enjoy its beauty, experience its power and risk its dangers. As Elisabeth Schüssler-Fiorenza has shown us, another tradition exists in the Hebrew canon and that is the Sophia tradition in which she places Jesus. It is a tradition in which power is shared and in this way increased. How ironic that Jesus who shared the power of embodied wisdom with those around him has since been imaged as the sole power holder, the one who alone has saved the whole world. Time to liberate this man and us all from those unequal tales.

Who would have thought that hearing the voices of women would have brought us this far! But wait, there's more! I've argued that theoretical change is possible and has liberating potential, but I am a feminist liberation theologian and so find myself wondering what real difference it will make.

Beyond Metaphysics – So What!

The demetaphysicsised Christ moves us away from creeds, doctrines and into a place of living documents – back to ourselves – as the ongoing narrative. Sophia's children are offered the chance to flourish, to dance within our own skins and, while we are having all this fun, to change the world. We are presented with an almost unique chance to expand

---

11. Joan Casanas quoted in Pablo Richard, *The Idols of Death and the God of Life* (Maryknoll, NY: Orbis Books, 198?), p. 122.

12. Daly, *Beyond God the Father*, p. 82.

the spaces that we share and to include all in the story of liberation and the praxis of redemption. Has Christianity ever before conceived a framework that gives it such a chance?

Nelle Morton challenged us to hear one another to speech and look how far we have come in accepting that challenge, but now we have to hear our bodies and the bodies of those we find repulsive, physically or morally — all have a piece of the picture. All bodies tell a story and the embodiment of feminist liberation theology requires that we create spaces in which people may begin to hear their own. Our praxis becomes fuelled by an enfleshed hermeneutic and we must become experts in 'reading the body'; this involves a variety of tools from psychology to economic theory since what goes on in them is as important as what happens to them under the weight of advanced capitalism.

As a woman I understand just how difficult this can be, deafened as we are by the disorientating babble of consumer cultures, patriarchal expectations and culturally constructed ideologies of gender. The female body is everywhere. We are not very clear about what it really is, but crystal clear about what it should be. What we do know, only because our sociologist friends have told us, is that the body is a site on which many discourses of power and knowledge are enacted. Indeed, we can find in very ancient philosophy the notion that the body was a means of diagnosis of social and political ills. Christianity has also been a player in this game and has made up discourses of its own about the female body, it has then to realise that it needs to find new ways of engaging with its own story telling if it is to be about life in abundance. Perhaps if we let roam the body of which Graham Ward speaks we can embrace more of the permeable and unstable nature of gender and even the self, and in so doing open up the whole theological arena and make something embodied happen!

We have begun this process — if imperfectly — by hearing and understanding that the body is situated differently within patriarchal society depending on what type it is; male/female, black/white, gay/straight, disabled/able bodied, the cosmos/humans. We have also become more subtle in our analysis understanding that class, economics, race, education and orientation are not as straightforward as we once thought and that they play a complex role in the way we are perceived and the way we perceive.

We have begun to, painfully, hear stories of abuse of the body through domestic violence, child abuse, war and the inhumane working conditions that advanced capitalism inflicts on us all but most devastatingly on those from the Third World. We all know that IMF stands for Immoral, Murdering Financiers (choose your own alternative!). It is good that we are finding ways to hear and developing modes of resistance and liberation praxis in the face of the reality unfolded in the stories. However, these are the 'big causes'. I remember when AIDS was first seen as a theological issue and we, quite rightly, had bleeding hearts and theological methods at the ready to deal with questions of those who contracted the virus 'innocently', through transfusions, as babies and even the odd misguided sexual act. But no sympathy and no theological method for the man who cruised up to 100 partners a weekend — why? Is he not incarnate too, does he not have a theological tale to tell? Was his life and the lives of thousands like him not a good enough site for the unfolding of incarnate truth? Yes, this is a big question but it is not a good one. The reverse is true when we come to the question of women — we are a good question but not a big one, that is there are always bigger ones and we can wait.

However, if the recent Women's Risk and AIDS Project[13] report is to be believed we are a big question. The female body is both being denied autonomy and is in denial in order to cope with this state of affairs. The report deals with young women and their experience of sexuality. It seems that, despite many years of feminist activism, sexuality is still a male dominated discourse — perhaps monologue. These women report framing their own sexual responses to please the male regardless of their own pleasure; being unable to insist on the use of condoms for fear of being labelled, and most worrying of all, not having a language in which to express their own understanding of sexuality — they had to use the male language if they tried to communicate at all on the subject. Heterosexuality then is more than a set of practices; it is a framework in which male domination underpins the generation of gender relations and the patriarchal society in which we live. It is as powerful as the church fathers feared. The study suggests that young women are under pressure to construct their bodies into a model of femininity that is inscribed on the surface by dress and make up, and is disembodied in that there is detachment from their own sensuality and alienation within their own skins.

The embodiment of feminist liberation theology under these circumstances is more than difficult. If in our most intimate relations we are being urged to become disembodied in order to fit in and meet the criteria, what is a girl to do? I said we should claim our desire and our erotic power as our divine birthright — rebel, embody alternate sexual strategies. Feminists have always known that the personal is political

---

13. See J. Holland, C. Ramazanoglu, S. Sharpe and R. Thomson, *The Male in the Head: Young People, Heterosexuality and Power* (London: The Tuffnell Press, 1998).

and Christians have always known that incarnation changes the world; if we combine the two we have a powerful mix.

One of my next projects will be developing the 'fat Jesus', the only one that currently exists is a Cuban cigar. There are, however, an increasing number of Slim for Him programmes which demonstrate, from the Bible, how anorexia is a holy path with experts assuring us that the gate is narrow, we have to pass through the eye of a needle, and Jesus was on a low fat diet of locusts, bread and honey. All these examples quoted to illustrate that only the skinny get into heaven. Narrow paradises again! It was always thus, especially if you were a woman—spiritual directors have long been advising women to 'disappear for Christ', be it by cutting off their breasts or starving themselves to the point where their periods stopped—this was hailed as having achieved the status of 'holy man of God'. Caroline Walker Bynum[14] and Rudolf Bell[15] have both shown how food has been understood differently for the sexes; men being encouraged to eat and women being encouraged to live on the host and die. Is it really any different today? Sociologists illustrate for us that it is not—food itself is gendered, as is the forum for consuming it.

Why are we fat women so problematic—we take too much space and we love it! Size matters. Big female bodies signify a moving beyond boundaries, we are transgressive and, if we refuse to be victimised, we are dangerous. There is a theology here of sacred space as resistance as well as gendered consumption which has huge implications both in the West and beyond; I am looking forward to writing it. The world cannot afford to lose any more women and so we need to realise that what is happening to, and within female bodies over issues of food is a sign of societal dysfunction and not individual moral weakness. Slim For Him—you must be joking!

Marcella Althaus-Reid[16] has called us to read theology through the bodies of the most marginalized and her suggestions are exciting and challenging. She brings before us as sites of theological reflection the drag Madonnas of Buenos Aires and, my favourite, Xena Warrior Christ. She urges us to write the theology of lovers and battered women and a Christology of prostitution; and of course we must if we are taking incarnation seriously, we cannot worry about decency. We have to embrace diversity in all its challenging forms. These stories have never been

---

14. Caroline Walker Bynum, *Holy Feast, Holy Fast. The Religious Significance of Food to Medieval Women* (Berkeley: University of California Press, 1987).
15. Rudolf Bell, *Holy Anorexia* (Chicago: University of Chicago Press, 1985).
16. Marcella Althaus-Reid, *Indecent Theology: Theological Perversions in Sex, Gender and Politics* (London: Routledge, 2001).

heard because they have been buried or purified by metaphysics. We have lived in a sanitised world from which we still wish to be saved! I am heartened and honoured to have Marcella[17] as my courageous companion on this next stage of the journey as we explore some of the hard questions together, the questions that even as feminists we have been reluctant to engage with.

Bodies tell stories, very complex and challenging stories; they are not all they seem and they surprise us at every turn. Ward points to transformations and boundary crossing as offering a salvific story/example in the life of Jesus why should it not be equally so in the theological telling of transsexual or transgendered people. Constructions of gender have, it seems, been too narrow; we keep walling in paradise, there is much more than we could ever image and we have not engaged with the unfolding of radical incarnation in these areas because we have refused to hear the stories and reflect on their meaning. Our vision has been narrowed by our fear—fear instilled by notions of dualism, perfection and ultimate ends. We don't have to embody the Greek virtues any more we simply have to embrace the risky, messy, muddled spiralling of incarnation. We do not need endpoints anymore but rather courage and imagination for engagement with our unfolding narratives.

Why Here? Why Now?

This would not be feminist liberation theology if I did not pay attention to my own context! It seems absolutely fitting that the first named post in feminist liberation theology should be at, embodied in, a Christian college. What other community can dedicate itself to counter cultural praxis in quite the same way? We are a community dedicated to incarnation as salvific and redemptive and so, by definition, it can be argued we are a community dedicated to risk, challenge, flourishing and taking seriously the divine/human reality of one another and our environment. We are then, in theory, a community with a vision, indeed with a vision that may seem out of step with those who don't hold the same basic principles to be true. Our Anglican Archbishop in Wales, Rowan Williams,[18] has recently gone on record asking Christians what they have to fear by exposing their faith to the world. Strangely, I find myself asking the same question. I am less generous than him in my assessment—we both

---

17. We are to be editors of a series exploring the way in which varying sexual preferences and performances of gender affect the creation of theology.

18. Rowan Williams has since been elected Archbishop of Canterbury. I dare to feel optimistic for the church!

agree that the praxis of Jesus can stand such exposure and will offer a vital challenge to this world of metanarratives and the war, exploitation and silencing that it spawns. But I am not sure that those who buy into the constructed faith will stand the test—they will be asked to give up so much; in my opinion all the right things such as power over and false status. They will be asked to look hard at Greek metaphysics and repent of the legacy that such Christianity has inflicted on the world. They will be asked to believe in something they have not yet seen, the empowerment, flourishing and godding of women, men and the planet. To pay homage to the once and for all son of God next to such a vision seems to have missed the point. The embodiment of feminist liberation theology is the antithesis to what the established churches have become. It cares little for rules and protocols but it is passionate about the lived reality of women and men. It has no power base to protect and so it is dangerous; dangerous enough to make a difference. With nothing to lose there is all to live for.

There seems no better time to live in such a way. We only have to look around to see where hierarchical thinking and policy making has led us. There is no better time to live as though, not simply to believe that, the power of God which courses through our veins has created a utopia/heaven, has created a place of mutuality and empowering relationality. Two 'Christian' world leaders are between them making plans which disregard the needy, exploit the planet, create in and out groups and consistently refuse to hear the voices of those whose lives they are affecting. What God is on their side? There is no better time to challenge this form of Christianity with its arrogance and neatly worked out game plan, no better time indeed to place the unfolding lives of women and men of all races and creeds at the centre of the creation of world economic policy, disputes over water or oil, questions of human rights and the integrity of the planet on which we all have to live. Marjon[19] is part of a global community, with students coming here from all over the world, and tutors from here going to all parts of the world. It is then uniquely placed to hear the voices of the marginalised and to gather their concerns as live issues within its own policymaking and its consultancy work with government and educational bodies. Institutions do have power and this Christian community can, at every turn, push back and offer alternatives; it can embody redemptive praxis.

A chair in feminist liberation theology should aim at being more than the solid unchanging structure on which scholars place arses it should be the ever-unfolding embodiment of challenging praxis. A platform from

19. Marjon or the College of St Mark and St John, Plymouth, UK.

which those who are marginalized can speak, not simply so that they can be heard, although that is a start, but in order that their concerns may fuel movements of resistance and add grist to our empowered imagination, that theses stories may help us as a community become an embodiment of hope and creative vision. Our feminist sisters hear to speech and our liberation brothers remind us that we are not here to pray for the world but to change it. A chair in feminist liberation theology then is a listening space dedicated to the full humanity and dignity of women and a highly politicised space understanding that alienation is not theoretical and so neither is liberation. It belongs to us all as a space in which to think differently and embody those thoughts in scholarship and critical/transgressive praxis. I am privileged to be working with students who through their own life experiences have formulated and are engaging with critical questions; questions that do not simply beg academic answers but rather inspire and propel us to other ways of seeing and of living. Thank you all. The college has honoured me with this chair in feminist liberation theology and my gift of thanks is to offer another way of looking, dedication of all my energies to the struggle of radical incarnation here amongst us and the courage to ask the hard questions. I hope I will not be alone!

Unlike Dr Martin Luther King Jr I have not been to the top of the mountain to see the Promised Land, I am a feminist theologian; I don't go in for elevation and distance! Instead I have looked at us all gathered here and I see the promised land, I see it in the grit and determination of the wearied campaigners, in the hopes and dreams of our young women, in the courage and resilience of us all—in our dreams, in our visions, our strength and our pain. I see it in our determination to keep telling our stories and to include more and more 'others' in that story telling. I see it in our struggles for bodily integrity. I see it in the desire to speak despite the will to silence exerted by those who believe they have power. I see it in claiming our narrative heritage and the way in which we expand that heritage through courageous living and stubborn resistance. I see it now because today is a good day, but sisters, when I become despairing do not let me flee to the comfort of redeemed eschatons and fluffy heavens, hold me back and remind me of the stories that are unfolding and the visions we strive for. Remind me of the revolutionary power of women living differently, keep me grounded and kindle my passion.

© The Continuum Publishing Group Ltd 2004.

'Pussy, Queen of Pirates':
Acker, Isherwood and the Debate on the Body in Feminist Theology

Marcella Althaus-Reid

> Our bodies and our sexuality are most our own but at the same time are the most taken away by all the edifices of patriarchy... Here it is a good place to start the revolution!
>
> Lisa Isherwood[1]

> Every position of desire, no matter how small is capable of putting into question the established order of society; not that desire is asocial, on the contrary. But it is explosive...
>
> Kathy Acker

Our Bushy Armpits: A Eucharist

If there was only one thing that we were allowed to claim in common, in these times of anti-essentialist discourse, it would be to say that in feminist theologies, the body always takes charge: our armpits come first. It is true that we are living at a time when both in the theological North Atlantic scene and in the Global South there are voices who would like to declare women's theologies either obsolete or too contradictory to be taken seriously. However, the presence of the body on the level of what one could call 'the materiality of feminist transcendence' gives feminist theologies a powerful grounded commonality of reflection which is neither obsolete nor divisive. In the midst of claims that feminism is dead in the post-modern era or too fragmented in different struggles to grant our praxis a common term such as 'feminist theology',[2] the sharing of the

---

1. Lisa Isherwood (ed.), 'Sex and Body Politics: Issues for Feminist Theologies', in *The Good News of the Body: Sexual Theology and Feminism* (Sheffield: Sheffield Academic Press, 2000), p. 21.
2. See, e.g., Ruth Page's neo-liberal dismissal of Feminist Theology by arguing that Feminist Theology (and feminism?) only had an 'interim nature' and that now the moment has come for women to do theology 'with men'. Cf. 'Has Feminist Theology a Viable Long-Term Future?', in D. Sawyer and D. Collier, *Is there a Future for Feminist Theology?* (Sheffield: Sheffield Academic Press, 1999), pp. 193-98. The academic forms

stories of our bodies remains as the location of gathering, of a communion and of eucharist in theology and in the church. The body, in feminist theology, is a very concrete issue of the kind that makes theology uncomfortable at times. A recent paper presented by Lisa Isherwood at the November 2001 meeting of the American Academy of Religion, reflecting on the theme of the body by reading Ensler's *The Vagina Monologues*,[3] illustrates this point. If the paper provoked uncomfortable feelings, that is usually the case with honest talk. However, Isherwood's paper succeeded precisely by its honesty and the perception that feminist theology has finally come of age.

In the presentation Isherwood made clear that in theology women's bodies count. Feminist theologies make our real bodies, what I would call our 'bushy armpits', count. That concrete transcendental presence of women's eucharist gathers together simultaneously spirituality and materiality and women's pleasure and conditions of work, combining them with the analysis of the sexual ideological construction of theology. The fact is that beyond the domesticated, shaved bodies of patriarchal theology, and the politics of limits imposed on women's theological thinking, there are armpits with glorious, rebellious chestnut bushy hair shouting out loudly their different stories. These stories make indecent, unfitting and transgressive theologies. In that sense we must remember that the starting point of our theologies are bodies, but the rebellious bodies: what Isherwood calls the body 'as is'[4] before theology starts to draw demonic and divine inscriptions in it.

The Body as Source and as Con/text

What we are saying here is that a woman's body is simultaneously source and context in theology. It is in the body 'as is' that we can find a pri-

---

of confrontation between feminist theology from the Global South, and feminist theology from the NorthAtlantic scene usually proceed along the lines of trying to assert who has suffered more, and who does a more 'realistic' (or useful) theology. As a theologian from the South living in Europe I can see that there are issues of both ignorance and romanticization of the Other in the theologies of both North and South. Usefulness, in theology, requires nuance. Not all women theologians from the South are committed to any particular struggle, while many European women theologians are committed to a degree of praxis and self criticism which is exemplary. There is commitment on both sides and also hypocrisy in both sides.

3. Lisa Isherwood, 'Indecent Theology: What F–ing Difference Does It Make?' paper presented for the panel on Indecent Theology, AAR 2001; repr. in *Feminist Theology* 11.2 (2003), pp. 141-47.

4. See Isherwood, 'Sex and Body Politics', pp. 20-34.

mary con/text and at the same time a hermeneutical circle: this is true equally for North Atlantic theologies and theologies from the Global South. The woman's body is the grounded experience of our theological praxis and as such a space to be theologically de-colonised.[5] I would like to add here that the political metaphor of de-colonisation is not only suggestive for the development of a political feminist project in theology but also to remind us of the complexity of issues of identity in feminist theology. Diasporic identities are hybrids that question the ideas of a natural model and exemplary norms for the body in theology and the theology grounded in it.

The concept I would like to reflect on in this paper is the concept of the divine body in relation to Isherwood's article 'Sex and Body Politics'. I have chosen this concept because it is significant and may hold the key for reflections about the future of feminist theologies. I would like to reflect on the divine body as what I would call 'cities of exiles'. This exilic quality seems to be present in more than one sense. First of all, cities of exile are places of liberative refuge, in the sense that the divine body becomes the original grounded 'divine signifier', or the space in which to be *Other*. That is to say that the divine body holds a space of possibility to deconstrain the body from the ideologies that rule the body in society, politics and theology. It is the space to be able to re-imagine ourselves, away from heterosexuality and other political bodily narrowness. In other words, there is a space of redemption to be found in the interstices between the place of God and women's bodies: such space makes of women's bodies a place of salvation.[6] There is here a theological opening up of sources and con/texts in theology. What happens is that we can read and be read by God in the midst of the concreticity of our history simply because God is inscribed in the passion and sufferings of concrete women's bodies. From this perspective it becomes evident that what feminist theologies have achieved in these last few years of a committed praxis of liberation, can be seen in their contribution to the restoration of the body in the discourse of the church and theology. Following on from this, the body which is a woman's body, is 'recreated' from the divine body in a movement of restoration; there is a giving back of the eucharist, or a return of gratitude, but only if we start with the body 'as is', a gratuitous, 'free' body. In other words, eucharist becomes

---

5. Isherwood, 'Sex and Body Politics', p. 21.
6. In this there is a relationship between this concept of the divine body and the work from late Uruguayan Roman Catholic theologian Maria Teresa Porcile Santiso, although Santiso lacks sexual analysis and it is constantly struggling to keep into the limits of a gender theology. See Porcile Santiso's book *La Mujer, Espacio de Salvación* (Madrid: Clarentianas, 1995).

freedom and gratitude as long communion starts by taking into account our bushy armpits and allowing them to become a site which also says something about God. That site is a source, an inspiration but it is also contextualised and grounded while admitting more than one reading of it.

Anybody There? On Sheep and Goats

'Is there a body in this room?' Graham Ward[7]

Doing feminist theologies in the 21st century is about good news and bad news. The bad news is that currently we have some divisive understandings of issues concerning the body and women's identities that have hermeneutical and practical implications in our feminist praxis. Also, our understanding of the body of God has developed in different directions. Basically, and at the risk of oversimplification, there is a division based on the 'gendered body' and the 'sexual body' as primary sources of theological reflection. In a rather provocative way, I have called these two different understandings the place 'where goats are divided from sheep'.[8] In that phrase I did not intend to make a moral or value judgement between gender theologians and sexual theologians (and in addition there are many combinations of these two positions), but rather to express my concern about the limitations that feminist theologies sometimes place upon the use of women's bodies as the context and source of our reflections. It is the issue of how far we can go, whether feminist theologies must end up with an analysis of cultural behavioural codes, or whether there can be something deeper than that.

Divisions and differences that do not contribute to dialogue are always bad news. However, the good news is that such apparent divisions are necessarily part of any type of 'doing theology' such as feminist theology. This happens simply because theologies of communion and eucharist (as liberationist theologies are, grounded in the materiality of the body) partake of the eucharistic ethos of scandal: and scandals are about the dividing and reuniting of the body divine to our bodies. Feminist theologies carry within them what Ward calls the eucharistic scandal that has to do with the identification of bodies, including their naming and issues surrounding their nature.[9] Ward paraphrases Stanley Fish by asking the

---

7. Graham Ward, *Cities of God* (London: Routledge, 2001).
8. 'Queer I Stand. Doing Feminist Theology outside the Limits of Colonial Decency', paper presented for the annual gathering of the European Society of Women in Theological Research, Salzburg, June 2001. ESWTR Yearbook 2002.
9. Ward, *Cities of God*, p. 83.

© The Continuum Publishing Group Ltd 2004.

question 'Is there a body in this room?' (or 'Is there a body in the Upper Room?') in order to be able to formulate the multitude of questions that the resurrection begs concerning the body. For our part, this is the moment in which to ask what kind of bodies are we dealing with in feminist theology, which is their past and present and also whether there is a future for those bodies.[10] In some circles the differences between women who stand by a theology informed by a gendered construction of bodies and those who gather around the sexual ideological conceptualisations may be considerable. At the risk of being accused of essentialism, I do believe that although there are different forms of theological praxis even amongst women who have left the gender paradigm out of their reflections, there is a major conceptual division in feminist theologies around issues of gender and sexuality. Such division does not mean enmity. There can be a clear and honest recognition that ecumenism may have a locus in a common practice of solidarity, without necessarily sharing a fixed conceptual position.

But how do we get this solidarity if there is no agreement on deeper issues of women's identity? How do we work ecumenically in the midst of this scandal? Here Isherwood provides a clue. By working from the concept of the body divine as a place of re-creation, she succeeds in extending the body. What we have here is a contribution towards the resolution of divisions in the past, in particular divisions of the late seventies and in the decade of the eighties, when feminist theologians appeared split along the lines that Isherwood calls the disagreement about how many bodies we have. Theologies at that time were constructed along the lines of the divisions between the political, the individual and the social body.[11] An example of this is the stereotype of women in the Global South, working along the lines of the political body (as political theologians) was contrasted with women in Europe who supposedly struggled for power in individual bodies ('individualist' theologians). The myth of the engaged versus the disengaged feminist theologian was created. The stereotype contained some truth (as does every stereotype) and much falsehood too, for bodies relate to each other in complex ways. Hence the 'individual body' theology gave birth in practice to a very political theological reflection concerning the body and the law, as in the case of translesbigay theologies. If the individual stereotype was contradicted in practice then we have to recognise on the other side that the discourse which began with a liberationist style of the 'political body' very often ended up in heterosexual idealism, failing to recog-

10. Ward, *Cities of God*, p. 83.
11. Isherwood, 'Sex and Body Politics', p. 22.

© The Continuum Publishing Group Ltd 2004.

nise the right of a woman to be 'not straight'.[12] Any of these emphases can become reductionist if they do not acknowledge their interrelation and mutual dependency. However, the stereotype has continued untill this day and has been particularly useful for that powerful branch of theology that is informed by heterosexual ideology: it can be used to disqualify feminist theologies as required. In fact, in the Global South many feminist scholars were and still are discounted by their main political co-theologians, while correspondingly in the North Atlantic scene the work of feminist theologians is dismissed for failing to exhibit the so-called 'Third World Women' approach.

It is interesting to note how the idea of the divine body could be useful here in providing a third space in which to re-imagine bodies (including dogmatic ones). This may be why the divine body is not a space in which we are fixed and immobile but, on the contrary, one for the dislocation of the sites of the body in theology. That is, the divine body becomes a place in which we can become larger, one in which we are able to assume in solidarity the experiences of *anOther* body even when its experiences are alien to us. Isherwood calls us to empower the divine body. However, an interesting point to make here is that it means to empower a God whose space dislocates fixed positions, a God who in the last instance, does not fit. Jesus seems a proper metaphor here for dislocation. Jesus, as the messiah who was out of place in so many contexts (political, cultural and religious) is the image of a God who does not fit and who calls us to be less troubled about fitting in and more concerned with extending our bodies with the experiences of others.

The Return of the Six Foot Tall Woman:
Empowering the Divine Body

Isherwood's theology comes out of her materialist vocation. She is a liberation theologian who exercises not only suspicion over the patriarchal meta-narratives of theological power, but who seeks to produce a discourse that empowers women and people marginalized by heterosexual theology. Together with Mary Hunt, Carter Heyward, Elizabeth Stuart, Naomi Goldenberg and many others, she pioneered a breakthrough in feminist theology by returning the body to Christian praxis. Such a breakthrough came even in the midst of other radical thinking in feminist theologies such as post-Christianity. But post-Christianity did not produce its promised *coup d'etat*, precisely because although it represents a radical

---

12. On this point, see my article 'El Derecho a no ser Derecha' (The Right not to be Straight), forthcoming in *Concilium* 298.5 (2002).

body theology it is still struggling against the limitations of gendered analysis. Influential as post-Christianity has been, Hampson's powerful attack on sexism and Christianity did not understand at that time that the genderised body, beyond being a meta-narrative of production, still conceals many surprises.[13] For instance, it hides the naturalisation of sexuality and its theological production, an analysis conceptualised later by Judith Butler and taken up by several theologians including this writer. Apart from that, the naturalisation of sexuality is usually bound to neo-liberalism. That is by the way, the contradiction to be found in many gendered theological discussions from the Global South. Feminist theologies there might claim to be politically socialist or even Marxist, but they can easily succumb to neo-liberalism and specifically to neo-conservatism when issues of women's identity are discussed. The feminist theological agenda of gender is usually developed to defend (heterosexual) family values and to encourage mediating structures for the promotion of the church as a civil society. The emphasis is on voluntary organisations and charity work is promoted as the main function of theology and church praxis. In this theological discourse, to be 'a woman' is something more or less known or at least, well guessed. It means somehow to be heterosexual, but even so heterosexuality is seldom discussed. Even if it were true that Hampson did not promote neo-conservatism in the form of family values, it is nevertheless the case that when there is an absence of any discussion on the heterosexual composite which constitutes theology there is always the danger of pre-empting issues of women' identity. Suffragette or housekeeper, unless there is an unmasking of the epistemological presuppositions of heterosexuality, the debate on women's identity will remain one of behaviourism, even if cultural differences in the prescription of women's behaviour are acknowledged. Somehow, Post-Christianity tends to kill the body by its strong gender position.

However, the idea of the larger than life divine body in the interstices of which there is a space for rebellions that are still grounded in real life acts as a corrective for reifications, especially as making of women's bodies mere sexual functions in theology. We need to remember that gender behaviourism is a tool in the formation of reification. The breakthrough produced by sexual feminist theologies represents, theologically, the return of the larger body or what we can call the 'Six foot tall woman'. (The reference is to an old and strange science fiction film permeated by the patriarchal fear of women's sizes.) It is the return of the body in feminist theology recognising that sexuality is a primal site for reification because sexuality does not happen in a power vacuum. What I should

13. D. Hampson, *Theology and Feminism* (Oxford: Basil Blackwell, 1990).

like now is, by using Goss' concept of 'theological accessorising',[14] to add some extra pieces to the wardrobe of the divine body of God, as a way of relating creatively to her work the experience of other bodies. Goss' accessoring concept is important because it seems to remind us that doing theology is a communitarian art and that by feeling free to take from our closets our own wardrobes of experiences we can join in solidarity with other people's theological journeys while reminding ourselves. As such, 'accessorising' is in the spirit of a theology struggling against essentialism, and trying to find a wider space for our theological praxis. Accessorising tells us to be more cautious with the concept of location in feminist discourse, in case it might prevent us from relativising other women's experiences simply because they are not ours.[15]

Acker and the Accessorising of God's Wardrobe in Feminist Theology

'I am looking for (a myth) where nobody else is looking'.[16]

I have chosen Kathy Acker's work to accessorise what might be one way forward for feminist theological thought, because there are some elements in her novels which are important for theology. Firstly, Acker consistently attempts to work out a language of the body in all her novels. While doing that she confronts honestly the problems and contradictions that come from thinking/writing from a woman's body—many of which are encountered by women doing theology. These pertain to issues of gender and sexuality and the inherited heterosexual logic of theology, especially in the role that the reader and the author play in a text.

Secondly, an important element in Acker's work is the way she deconstructs texts that have become meta-narratives of authority. When Acker deconstructs important texts and enables them to relate to others, she is usually confounding fact and fiction in a somewhat messy way, showing in this way the ambiguities and contradictions of how our bodies have been positioned contradictorily in heterosexual ideologies. And thirdly, Acker works with a premise that relates closely to our reflections upon the concept of the divine body. Hampson, as Daly before her, has pow-

---

14. For Goss's concept of accessorising in theology see his book *Queering Christ: Beyond Jesus Acted Up* (Cleveland, OH: Pilgrim Press, 2002), and also Marcella Althaus-Reid's '"Obscenity no. 1: Bi/Christ": Expanding Christ's Wardrobe of Dresses', *Feminist Theology* 11.2 (2003), pp. 157-66.

15. See Isherwood, 'Sex and Body Politics', p. 24, for comments about location and reductionism in feminist theology.

16. See http://www.centerforbookculture.org/interviews/interview_acker.html (Ellen Friedman, 'A Conversation with Kathy Acker').

erfully disclosed the fact that Christianity cannot avoid the omnipresence of the Phallus (which both conflagrated with the penis). Without a sexual theology to back her thinking, this represented for Hampson the end of the road for any feminist theology. Acker also thinks that women cannot hide from the presence of the Phallus but she looks for myths in the sense of what I have called the cities of exile that the body divine can provide. This is the myth of a lesbian phallus,[17] or of a discourse that could undercut the privileging of the penis in the positioning of the Phallus. Hampson's theology starts and ends in this basic point: the lack of choice that the presence of the Phallus gives us in Christianity. And I deliberately say 'us' in a non-specific way here, since it is not only women who are subjected to this regime: apart from translesbigays, heterosexual people including men are oppressed by this Phallochratic regime. However, at this point, like Acker, we may have an exit at hand, a place to go, or places to be dreamt and to be taken seriously in theological praxis. For as we have seen before, this divine body is a unique space for transgression and recreation, although the divine body is not constructed here as a fixed location. Instead of that we are reflecting on a divine body that dis-locates us (allowing us a fresh search for our bodies' identities) but also dislocates God up to the point that a new kenotic movement is required. Our finding of the divine body as cities of exile requires the exile of God too, but this time, in ourselves.

That is when Acker's novel, *Pussy, King of the Pirates* becomes interesting for us, because in it Acker is also trying to construct her own divine body in the sense that she wants to construct a utopia for re creational purposes. For Acker, constructing a utopia is a task related to sign making; that is, to make our own signs in a society where the presence of the Phallus is so permissive as to be unavoidable.[18] In *Pussy, King of the Pirates* Acker works with the myth of the pirate world that deals with the construction of identity through race, gender, sexuality and political co-ordinates. The pirate's myth is that of the third space, a chaotic space that transgresses what Acker has previously described as *borderdome*, an allusion to the tired limits of fixed heterosexual discourses.

At this point we can see the similarities between the concept of the divine body and Acker. In *Pussy, King of the Pirates*, the character of Pussy (or Pussycat) achieves the glory of becoming herself, that is, 'the king of her body', by following a strategy of re-positioning desires. Pussy's desires move fast and chaotically in Acker's novel to the point that desires need to be re-fitted constantly. Pussy's sexuality is difficult

17. Judith Butler, *Bodies that Matter* (London: Routledge, 1993), p. 84.
18. See Friedman, 'A Conversation with Kathy Acker', p. 5.

to fix. The divine body could also be described as a space in constant refitting exercise, in the sense that in it we, outcasts and pirates of the world, could be re-imagining and re-desiring our bodies. As women, we know that we do not fit the constructions of the body that Christianity has provided us with. However, God does not fit them either. A theological accessory here could be feminist fetishism. If the fetish is there to substitute the Phallus, the divine body needs to be understood in fetish terms because it is positioned here for the same fetish reasons. The divine body cannot be a supplement, because it cannot add to anything; it should not supplement or add to anything since there are no originals here. However, the divine body could be a trace of the unknown loving/knowing theological source which fetishism, with all its ambiguity and undecidability, seems to foresee. As in Acker, such theological inquiry would require us to de-familiarise ourselves with the language of the body in theology and acquire a new language. Isherwood, in her reflections on the *The Vagina Monologues* gives us a powerful example of this when, using Goldenberg's concept, she speaks in terms of the divine masquerade of Christianity[19] which needs to be resisted, to avoid being co-opted into the male divine system of signification. Reflecting perhaps in a similar mood, Acker puts these words into the mouth of Ostracism, one of the female characters in *Pussy, King of the Pirates*: 'The closer I became to Pussycat, the more her obedience to paternal authority, specially in its absence, made no sense'.[20]

Extending the Divine Vagina

In Isherwood, the vagina of the 'monologues' also becomes a divine space that should be preserved from patriarchal philosophical penetrations. So Isherwood denounces powerfully those feminist theologians who still look for grace in the patriarchal theology and language that has abused women. The vagina is a theological locus to be privileged, as a place to be and to have, in order to start reflecting on God and the body 'as is'. As a theological extension, the vagina dislocates the theological Phallus by taking away the Phallus of God the Father as the privileged subject or maker of the law. Therefore, in this extension of the divine body (which is also a displacement of the Phallus) the fetishist epistemology that accessorises feminist theological wardrobes is already present in the concept of the divine body. The divine body is a space of extension, of enlarging and recreating our bodies and sexualities. At the same time, we are the

---

19. Isherwood, *Indecent Theology*, p. 40.
20. Kathy Acker, *Pussycat Fever* (Edinburgh: AK Press, 1995), p. 42.

extension of that divine body; a divine body which is to be found in a vagina. This is crucial for as Isherwood reminds us in her reflections on the vagina, which is extended in 'a glorious communion of menstrual blood, that internal/external eschatological promise, the bloody reminder of incarnational potential and celebratory waiting'.[21] Fetishism, with its capacity to gather conflicts, as for instance knowledge and desire[22] in feminist theologies can become a strategy for rethinking the divine in this context and forcing the divine to rethink too. The in- betweenness that Acker searches for in *Pussy, King of the Pirates*, deconstructs theology (and systematic theology) powerfully, almost heretically.

For Acker, it is crucial to find a new language to express what has not and cannot be said: the undecidable. She works through the creation of a language which can reflect the fluency of sexual identities, through the chaos of non-linear scripts[23] and the deconstruction of central identities. In her novel *Pussy, King of the Pirates*, Ostracism discovers pirate sex by affirming what Butler calls the presence of the lesbian phallus. And she achieves that by messing around in her narrative with the penis, by devaluing the penis as the place to have the phallus, that is, to have the law, the discourses of authority. The messing around is in order to be makers, not receivers of the law.

The challenges presented here to feminist theologies are many and crucial. Feminist theologies need to reflect more on the concept of the divine body, in order to ground a theology of the body 'as is'. For that it is necessary to find new non linear ways of writing feminist theology and to engage in serious deconstructions of Systematic Theology. At the end of the day, we all must remember the words from Pussycat: ' First, I have to get away from daddy'.[24] Or as Isherwood says: 'we need to stop finding places in an already worked out theology, one that brings us back to the fathers and the disquiet of denial and the safety of daddy's arms'.[25] Let us continue then accessorising body theologies with the courage and theological honesty required for dogmatic bodies to become larger and non-fitting, and in the process, to rediscover God and communion—extending our bodies and extending the bodies of God.

---

21. Isherwood, *Indecent Theology*, p. 8.
22. E.L. MacCallum, *Object Lessons. How to do Things with Fetishism* (Albany: State University of New York). See also 'How to do Things with Fetishism', in *Differences* 7.3 (http://www.iupjournals.org/differences/dif7-3.html).
23. Kathy Acker, *Bodies of Work: Essays*, 'Serpent's Tail' (1997).
24. Acker, *Pussycat Fever*, p. 43.
25. Isherwood, *Indecent Theology*, p. 5.

© The Continuum Publishing Group Ltd 2004.

A Theology of Corporeality Embodied in the Butch Femme[1] Bar Culture of the 1950s and 1960s

Marie Cartier

ABSTRACT

It is my intention in this brief study to extend the argument that Nestle begins with her seminal article, 'Butch-Femme Relationships: Sexual Courage in the 1950s', and that Henking and Comstock continue by including it in the critical anthology of writings on 'being queer' and 'being religious', *Qu(e)erying Religion*. I want to do this by making 'an overt claim' that the butch-femme community of the 1950s (actually this community is active from the 40s through the early 60s) created its own spirituality — in the content of a corporeal theology between couples and individually, and that these couples/individuals were also part of this larger 'bar community' that created a space for the community to refine this theology in terms of self-defining community. I want to argue that this self-defined community served to function for its members in many of the same ways any religious community functions that is held together by a common faith and/or theology.

> ...I praise those hands, with scars she's proud of,
> on gender fuck forearms.
> They steady my pulse,
> *settle down, settle down,* curve on my cheek
> in the dark like a prayer.
>
> ...Her hands say yield and make it sound safe.
> They enter me like something holy.
>
> It takes time to interpret the tongue of her hands,
> the whispering of 'come here',
> or the bunch and knot of 'back off ',
> as they churn cement, hoist bricks,
>
> sludge mortar into cracks,
> knife off the excess,
> until she's built Jericho
> and I have no trumpet...

1. I use 'femme' while Kennedy and Davis use 'fem', the spelling favoured in the 1950s.

> ...I am in the sweet, inquisitive poultice
> of her hands,
> proudly helpless, wanted, given.
> She makes loaves and fishes of me.[2]

Introduction

By re-framing the gaze on theology/spirituality, it is possible to re-vision the reason why this community was and remains so important to contemporary lesbians, and also to allow us a possible re-interpretation of the experience of the butch-femme community—in their own words.

What I have found is that many of the basic functions of a faith community—weekly meetings, commitment to a theology—in this case a praxis of sacred corporeality, commitment to the members of the community, shared ideology, refusal to deny identity, and willingness to endure extreme danger of one's physical being/psyche in order to continue to practise one's 'faith' and ensure 'communal survival', were all present in the bar culture of the 50s.

While I do not want to claim an identity that is not historically authentic, I do believe that I have found from studying this population, that there is a verifiable model of theology present in its functioning. Because this community functioned illegally, diaries, letters, and the type of resources usually looked at by a historian are not readily available. In lieu of these sources, I interviewed the few women of the many I contacted that agreed to the interview. In addition I used period fiction, poetry and prose of well-known authors of this period and culture— among them, Leslie Feinberg, Dorothy Allison, Chyrstos, Joan Nestle and Judy Grahn. I also utilized period articles, magazines, and some histories such as Ann Aldrich's *We Walk Alone,* as well as contemporary creative writing and critical interpretations of gender and specifically butch femme gendering.

Which Theological Model?

It is by utilizing the hermeneutical approach of gay theology that we begin to see the possibility for locating a theology within bar culture.

> If the word 'theology' can at all be salvaged in our era, theology can no longer be thought an exclusively—or even primarily—a church matter, but should rather be thought of as the public enterprise of taking stock in

---

2. Smyth, Cherry, 'Loaves and Fishes', in Sally Munt (ed.), *Butch-Femme: Inside Lesbian Gender* (London: Cassell, 1998), pp. 47-49.

which an individual or a culture reflects critically on its direction in life. Likewise gay theology is not the clarification of what the churches and synagogues have taught and do teach about homosexuality, but rather the exploration of what can and should be said religiously on the basis of gay experience, thereby making a distinctively gay contribution to the general discussion.[3]

This praxis of 'faith seeking understanding' then in terms of gay theology should not be defined in the 'academic' setting of the church hierarchy, but within the believing community *itself*—as a public enterprise of that culture's reflection on its direction. In addition, since theology is not about seeking final answers, it is appropriate that its primary praxis is exploration, rather than formal teaching. Corporeal theology would then be theology or practice done within a believing community that is 'characteristic of the body', or 'tangible'.

> ...recently religious ethicist and feminist theorists, both religious and secular, have challenged us to rethink our negative attitudes toward sexuality and spirituality. Much of this work has employed the term 'embodiment', a recognition that as human beings we are embodied beings and cannot separate our physical existence from our spiritual. All human beings may have a soul, but as human beings we cannot know this part of ourselves divorced from our physical bodies. The part of Western Christianity which has proclaimed the subordination of the body to the soul as the paradigm of spiritual excellence denies that which makes spiritual awareness possible in this world, our flesh and blood existence.[4]

The idea of an embodied spirituality, resting in a corporeal praxis, is highlighted in the work of several contemporary gay and lesbian theologians/religious writers, as well as heterosexual writers. Among them are the Reverend Nancy Wilson (*Our Tribe: Queer Folks, God, Jesus and the Bible*), James Nelson (*Body Theology*), Riane Eisler (*Sacred Pleasure*), Alison Webster (*Found Wanting: Women, Christianity and Sexuality*), and Andrew Harvey (*The Gay Mystics*).

This Christian view is re-enforced I believe, particularly for women, by the contemporary writings on religions commonly known to embody corporeal practice, such as tantric Buddhism.[5] This correlation will be drawn more strongly further into this article.

---

3. Ronald E. Long, 'The Sacrality of Male Beauty and Homosex: A Neglected Factor in the Understanding of Contemporary Gay Reality', in David Gary Comstock and Susan E. Henking (eds.), *Qu(e)erying Religion: A Critical Anthology* (New York: Continuum, 1993), p. 280.

4. Say, A. Elizabeth and Mark R. Kowalewski, *Gays, Lesbians and Family Values* (Cleveland, OH: Pilgrim Press, 1998), pp. 75-76.

5. Miranda Shaw, *Passionate Enlightenment: Women in Tantric Buddhism* (Princeton, NJ: Princeton University Press, 1994).

© The Continuum Publishing Group Ltd 2004.

For now, suffice it to say, that several theologians have spoken of an embodied theology for lesbians and gay men that employs corporeal praxis, and that this theology should be drawn from the lived experience of the community itself.

What Is a 'Shared Identity?'

Identity is defined as 'the collective aspect of the set of characteristics by which a thing is definitely recognizable', or 'the set of behavioural characteristics by which an individual is regarded as a persistent entity'.

To 'share' an identity is 'to participate, use, or experience in common', that identity. To be a community with a 'shared identity' means then that community participates in a 'collective aspect', sharing and or *using* behavioural characteristics to become recognizable members of that group.

> Religion is thus not to be understood exclusively as a relation with a worshipful 'god',—but rather as one's relations with any revered reality. It follows, then, that a group's or an individual's religious life is pluriform—constelled by the multiplicity of things revered and whatever pattern of hierarchy in which those realities are ordered which may or may not include a relation with a morally perfect sacred reality.[6]

So, then when I speak of religion, theology, community, sacrality, I am not speaking necessarily exclusively, but rather re-framing my gaze perhaps on what constitutes 'revered reality', and suggesting that the praxis of a sacred life, may or may not include interaction with a 'morally perfect' reality.

> This is an important point, for when I claim that being gay is religious in character, I am not claiming that being gay is *the* religion of gay men. Gay life is not a cult in that sense—nor does it involve the recognition of a sacrality that is 'jealous' of other sacred realities. Rather, while the valuation of male beauty and homosex that anchors gay life is itself religious it is a reverential tie that will probably take its place among other sacred ties.[7]

There are some contradictions here with lesbian life, especially as evidenced in butch/femme culture but, for this juncture, what is important is that when I attempt to articulate a theology of this period, it by no means connotes that by adopting this 'theology', the community dissolved all other 'sacred ties'.

---

6. Long, 'The Sacrality of Male Beauty and Homosex', p. 275.
7. Long, 'The Sacrality of Male Beauty and Homosex', p. 275.

The Butch Femme Community as Theological Model

> All commentators on twentieth century lesbian life have noted the prominence of butch–fem roles. Before the 1970s their presence was unmistakable in all working-class lesbian communities, the butch projected the masculine image of her particular time period at least regarding dress and mannerisms — and the fem, the feminine image, and almost all members were exclusively one or the other. Buffalo was no exception. As in most places, butch–fem roles not only shaped the lesbian image but also lesbian desire, constituting the base for a deeply satisfying erotic system.
>
> …Eventually we came to understand that these (roles) were at the core of the community's culture, consciousness and identity. For many women, their identity was in fact butch or fem, rather than gay or lesbian.[8]

As Kennedy and Davis explain, when they began the research for their history of *Boots of Leather, Slippers of Gold*, they thought that butch-femme roles would be incidental and marginal, as had been suggested by many others. Lillian Faderman in the book hailed as 'the definitive study of modern lesbian life', *Odd Girls and Twilight Lovers*,[9] suggests that 'butch women *would not* be covert and the femmes who *let* themselves be seen with them often led dangerous lives'. Her writing carries an implicit charge against overt expression of the butch femme model. Instead of seeing these roles at the core of a developing community, she sees them as marginal, and detrimental to that development:

> They courted violence. Many of them were certainly courageous in their insistence on presenting themselves in ways that felt authentic, but their bravery made them victims. Heterosexuals could stand neither the idea of a woman usurping male privilege…nor a sexuality that totally excluded them. Their outrage often took the form of physical violence.
>
> ….middle and upper-class lesbians could be comforted by the presence of policemen…but butch-fem couples did not have the luxury of that illusion.
>
> …middle and upper-class lesbians had to cope with…the preposterous images of lesbians in the media, but generally their 'discreet' style allowed them to carry on their existence without molestation.[10]

It is not my intention here to validate necessarily the butch-femme community or to valorise it. In many respects, that work has been done

---

8. Elizabeth Lapovsky Kennedy and Madeline D. Davis, *Boots of Leather, Slippers of Gold: The History of a Lesbian Community* (New York: Routledge, 1993), p. 5.

9. Lillian Faderman, 'Butches, Femmes and Kikis: Creating Lesbian Subcultures in the 1950s and 60s', in *Odd Girls and Twilight Lovers* (New York: Columbia University Press, 1991), pp. 158-87.

10. Faderman, 'Butches, Femmes and Kikis', pp. 184-85.

by Kennedy and Davis, and was the driving force of their twelve year study. They excellently create the community histories that support that butch-femme roles were not marginal, that they were the majority, that they were not 'optional' therefore it was not that butches 'would not' conform to societal expectations, it is that they 'could not'. This has been borne out by my own research.

I want here to only briefly support their re-interpretation with the following.

A 70-plus-year-old narrator that I interviewed said that she was 'stone butch until about fifteen or twenty years ago...' and said the following of her 'role':

> ...butch...femme...it's what goes beyond sex...it goes into your whole being...it's part of your whole make up...even though I'm butch sexually...my sex is only part of this...but being butch is how I am, how I feel...[11]

By 'stone butch' the narrator means that she would not let her lover penetrate her, or possibly make love back to her. She has changed this because of her lover's desire, not her own.

> I always made love to them, and I always got a thrill out of it... I enjoy being on top. You know what I mean? Being the one who's overtly sexual...[12]

In recent years, she conceded she had stopped this practice, and let her lovers be more overtly sexual with her.

The issue of the 'stone butch' is a very interesting conception, especially if we consider it in the light of a new theological model of corporeality originating within the people it serves. I will deal more with this idea further in the study.

It is beyond the scope of this study to analyse all of the intricate gendering of the butch-femme relationship; and its predecessors and antecedents. From this author's research, it appears that butch women themselves do not feel mutable, or marginal, but feel permanently marked on the landscape of gay and lesbian history; and that they were the strongest agents of a movement for gay and civil rights. This position is supported by the research of Kennedy and Davis. For while the small, educated homophile movement was gathering strength for 'assimilation', the butch and femme were aggressively claiming and holding space in large and visible numbers.

11. Flo Fleishman, Personal Interview with Author, Los Angeles, CA, September 1998.
12. Fleishman, Personal Interview with Author, 1998.

© The Continuum Publishing Group Ltd 2004.

I agree with Kennedy and Davis, that it is much harder to find and therefore interview femme women of the period. Femme women have been ridiculed as 'tools of patriarchy' and not allowed ownership of their story as one of historic consequence. Because as a people we lock ourselves into a binary position of gendering whether it is masculine, feminine, butch or femme, it is difficult to place the femme woman who owns femininity within the female lesbian body as different than the female who owns femininity within the heterosexual body. Therefore it becomes problematic to encode her historical significance of the butch-femme movement in terms of 'courage' — because after all, the 'only' thing she was doing differently than a heterosexual woman...dating a masculine looking woman, 'letting herself be seen with..."butches"...'

I would like to suggest that this was however a radically transgressive act. It is in this act, and that of the gendering of the stone butch that much of the 'theology' that I would like to propose will originate.

It seems obvious to this author that butch and femme, while they are owned individually, are relational terms, primarily indicating a sexual position or desirous of one. So, it stands to reason that without 'femme', 'butch' loses much of its potency.

> The two most public lesbian genders are butch and femme. Whether as the singular categories butch and femme, or as the 'co-dependent' entity butch/femme...these lesbian genders have facilitated lesbian sex, lesbian desire for decades. Butch femme has become a form of self-representation for lesbian; it gives lesbian desire a partial sometimes reluctant entry into the symbolic realm of language and culture. In the hegemonic sense, we are women, but we are something else too.[13]

The following quotes are from self-identified femme authors who lived during the period and serve as illustration of their self-placement on this landscape, and not with the conscription that they were 'letting' themselves, as Faderman suggests, be coupled with butches, but for the most part, that they saw themselves as courageous partners, not victims, in the dance.

> I fly to you
> To be soothed in the wings
> of your Butch tenderness
> hidden under fierceness necessary as mine
> to ride your feathers, fingers & tongue...[14]

---

13. Munt, *Butch/Femme*, p. 4.
14. Chrystos, 'I Fly to You', in *Fire Power* (Vancouver, Canada: Press Gang Publishers, 1995), p. 52.

I do like tough women, butch women, big, confident, strong women... I like to scream when I feel the burning heat of her skin on mine. It is then that every part of me opens and sound naturally happens, the sounds not of passion but of joy. Satisfaction. Determined grown-up satisfaction that denies silence, all silences, most particularly the long silence of my girlhood, the denial of a lesbian girlhood, the denial of a lesbian girl-child who was never meant to survive.[15]

I wanted her to see my competent femme self, self-supporting and sturdy, and then I wanted her to reach under my dress, to penetrate the disguise I wore in a world that saw me as having no sexuality because I had no boyfriend or husband... Here now on the bed, all the offerings would be tested...we both had power in our hands. She could turn from me and leave me with my wetness, my need...a vulnerability and a burden. I could close up, turn away from her caring and her expertise. But neither happened. We kissed for a few minutes and soon her hands knew I was not afraid... I strained to take and give to her, to pour my wetness in gratitude upon her...her hands and lips. I have never felt so beautiful... She reached deep into me, past the place of coming, into the centre of my womanness.[16]

I come to orgasm from your fullness... In ten years of marriage to a man I never came to this from the pleasure of him inside me. There was always elaborate manipulation of me by him. But you are excited by my desire... You are a woman who has been accused of betraying womanhood... Traitors to our sex, or spies and explorers across the boundaries of what is man, what is woman? My body yawns open greedily for what you are not afraid to give me.[17]

A butch woman once came up to me after a performance of my one woman show, *Ballistic Femme*, in which I explore the dynamics of the butch-femme relationship from a contemporary perspective, and she told me that the following lines made her 'proud — because someone finally got it'.

The first butch woman took that scarf of need and ate it like thanksgiving and for the first time, for the first time, for the first time... I was no longer ashamed...for the first time I was no longer ashamed.[18]

What is being received? What did I 'get'? What is 'the place of foreign knowledge' that the butch and femme go to? What I am suggesting is

---

15. Dorothy Allison, 'Femme', in *Skin: Talking About Sex, Class and Literature* (Ithaca, NY: Firebrand Books, 1994), p. 152.
16. Joan Nestle, 'Esther's Story', in *A Restricted Country* (Ithaca, NY: Firebrand Books, 1995), pp. 43-44.
17. Minnie Bruce Pratt, 'Mimosa', in *S/He* (Ithaca, NY: Firebrand Books, 1995), pp. 117-18.
18. Marie Cartier, *Ballistic Femme* (upublished), p. 21.

that where one goes, what one gets, or 'got' in the context of historical or contemporary butch-femme participation was the definition of and community based on, a theology, as defined by corporeal praxis.

While I realise that...

> ...the experience including the sexual experience, of every human being in every time and place is distinct from that of every other human being, and that the social matrix in which she or he lives will determine that experience in a largely irresistible way, including creating (or not creating) opportunities for sexual expression and possibly even awareness of sexual feelings and desires.[19]

I believe that it is possible to draw similarities between theology, butch-femme bar culture of the 50s and butch-femme contemporary culture, without doing a disservice to either the traditional definition of theology, or to the historic or contemporary cultures.

What Was This Community's Shared Identity?

> For gender to be recognized it has to be shown to another person. Hence gender relies upon being performed. It is the playing out of specific characteristics that are then recognized and classified as either the feminine or the masculine.[20]

In terms of a shared identity, one thing becomes apparent—that performing gender is a requisite and shared praxis. From the statements from femmes and butches this praxis had to do with sexual loving that took the participants to another 'place', the 'centre', sexuality that was transcendent.

> I didn't learn much about butch femme being just 'lesbian', or about having strength in relationships...butch femme contributes a lot of the concept of relationships and how people work together... I have more respect for women, and for femmes now... I have a better understanding ...Butch femme relationships give me the freedom to be me...and...femmes appreciate me being me...my body, my size and strength...it's appreciated by femmes...[21]

---

19. John Boswell, 'Concepts, Experience and Sexuality', in David Gary Comstock and Susan E. Henking (eds.), *Qu(e)erying Religion: A Critical Anthology* (New York: Continuum, 1993), p. 117.

20. Michelle Atherton, 'Feminine and Masculine Personas in Performance: Sade Huron: A Drag Queen with a Dick', in Nina Rapi and Maya Chowdhry (eds.), *Acts of Passion: Sexuality, Gender and Performance* (London: Haworth Press, 1998), p. 230.

21. 'Amazon Nan' (pseudonym), Personal Interview with Author, 28 December 1998, Los Angeles, California.

© The Continuum Publishing Group Ltd 2004.

In other sources, butches also talk about sharing technique (that is, information on praxis) with each other. And femmes talk about sharing information with each other, and specifically about teaching butches praxis—or how to make love. If we can say that there is tangible corporeal embodied theology present in this community, then it is being developed within the community itself, and passed to its members by its members.

> I realised she was looking for a dildo. I couldn't remember anything Al had taught me—not a word. All I remembered was Jacqueline's warning: *You could make a woman feel real good with it or you could make her remember all the ways she's ever been hurt.*[22]

I would finally like to suggest, that this theology of the body is passed perhaps mainly from femmes to butches, and to make a rather large theological leap—to suggest that this is perhaps the same *type* of information in the tantric tradition of Buddhism on transcendental praxis that was passed from women to men, from femininely gendered beings to masculinely gendered beings; and that these women, in both cultures, *could be* considered sacred bearers of knowledge.

> The secret oral instruction that these women gave included the inner yogas that form the basis of the sexual practices. Several of the accounts relate that after receiving the esoteric instructions, the yogi in question was accepted as a consort by a female Tantric and proceeded to practise with her, in some cases for several months and in others for many years.[23]

What appears to be the authentic passing of sexual expertise in terms of love making to a woman's body, appears to come from this research from women, rather than from men. Women know and pass on this knowledge—the feminine holds this sacred knowledge, and then imparts it to the masculine—only who seek it out/search for it.

This type of knowledge—how to actually and really make love to a woman—is not usually sought by men, but apparently is sought by *masculinely gendered* women, that is butches.

What does it mean to create a community where the sexuality of women is honoured? Outside of the butch femme contemporary community, and historical community, the intense 'worship' of female desire cannot easily be found in *community*, except for the aforementioned example of tantric Buddhism.

---

22. Leslie Feinberg, *Stone Butch Blues* (Ithaca, NY: Firebrand Books, 1993), pp. 71-72.
23. Miranda Shaw, *Passionate Enlightenment*, p. 180.

> ...in the second half of the nineteenth century the emerging medical profession gave scientific sanction to traditional homosexual behaviour... the mannish lesbian proved a potent persona...her image came to dominate the discourse about female homosexuality...
>
> ...sexual desire was not considered inherent in women, the lesbian was endowed with a trapped male soul that phallicized her, giving her active lust.
>
> ...It was Richard Kraft Ebing who articulated the fusion of masculinity, feminist aspiration and lesbianism that became and largely remains an article of faith in Anglo-American culture.[24]

If it is an 'article of faith' that sexual desire cannot be held in a woman actively, but only in a masculinely gendered woman, what does it mean to live in an opposing culture like butch femme where sexual desire in femininely gendered women is expected, and then honoured? I am suggesting that this type of alternate 'faith' begins to constitute a radical theology of difference—a corporeal theology rooted in sexual praxis designed to bring the genders, in this case both embodied in the biological female, into union with one another.

One could draw a comparison here to tantra, and possibly an analogy to the union of human with the divine—especially when 'human' is seen as 'man' (generic), and God (Divine as Holy Spirit, or female) through the Eucharist. The Eucharist and its sacrament being an embodied experience—you 'eat the body, drink the blood', therefore entering into union with Divinity, Christ (male), but also then filled with 'the Holy Spirit' (female).

It is possible that some femmes saw themselves this way. Evidence is there in the quotes, but much more research would have to be done to formulate an accurate picture of the 'theology' of this group—if it is 'real' that this did exist on some level, and is not merely post-modern speculation.

Certainly a contemporary reading indicates this worship/worshipper speculation as more probable that not.

> My femme friend F. says to me, 'What I like about femmes is they're like queens'. 'Queens?' I say. I think of crowns and sceptres, regal women staring imperiously from thrones... 'You know *queens*', she says, 'Drag queens'. Femmes are dykes in girl-drag. 'Oh, that kind of queen', I say, 'yes of course, you're right'. Both meanings merge as I contemplate myself as femme, deliberately cross-dressing myself in femininity as drag, construct-

---

24. Esther Newton, 'The Mythic Mannish Lesbian: Radclyffe Hall and the New Woman', in Martin Bauml Duberman, Martha Vicinus and George Chauncy, Jr (eds.), *Hidden from History: Reclaiming the Gay and Lesbian Past* (New York: New American Library, 1989), p. 287.

ing myself as a spectacle for women's eyes. Queen of the Night. Queen of Desire. The woman to be desired who declares herself a desirer of women. Queen femme.[25]

'Rules' for Enduring Danger

Of course, when we talk about butch femme, we must acknowledge that we are talking about a people under siege—nightly bar raids by police, gang rape, beatings by heterosexual men were all part and parcel of the experience of being part of this community (see Kennedy and Davis, Feinberg and Nestle for documentation)—but we are also talking about the 'perks', the new 'in your face' sexual freedom and what I want to call here, the ability to belong to a 'new Church'—that of butch-femme.

Research has been done to ensure partly this community's resurrection from its marginal placement that Fadermen initially assigned it. Obviously we would not, in retrospect, suggest that African-American's obvious attempts at civil rights by participating in overt action, such as sit-ins, made them 'victims' but heroes. This type of re-framing around the butch-femme community has begun and continues. It also becomes more important for the contemporary lesbian to—especially gendered butch and/or femme—have a sense of, and demand a re-reading of, this history.

> ...the time period of the fifties...it sets the stage for the freedom we have now...(it's important to) put it in people's faces so that they have to see it.[26]

What this study suggests is that heroic action was necessary for the survival of something this community believed in—something that they could not have found elsewhere—such as in the 'discreet' lifestyle of the homophile middle-class movement. What they were standing their ground for, in the face of severe life-threatening harassment, I am suggesting was the ability to love with 'persistent desire'.[27]

The butch, even the 'stone butch', is desired and wanted, as is the femme—the masculine woman whose desire is to 'please' and the feminine woman whose function in the dryad is to be 'pleased'. I put 'please' in quotes, because 'pleasure' is an ambiguous term—if what you desire to do *is please*, then you are *being pleased* in that action.

---

25. Wendy Frost, 'Queen Femme', in Leslea Newman (ed.), *The Femme Mystique* (Los Angeles, CA: Alyson Publications, 1995), p. 303.

26. 'Amazon Nan' (pseudonym), Personal Interview with Author.

27. Elizabeth Lapovsky Kennedy, 'The Hidden Voice: Fems in the 1940s and 50s', in Laura Harris and Elizabeth Crocker (eds.), *Femme: Feminists, Lesbians and Bad Girls* (London: Routledge, 1997), pp. 15-16.

© The Continuum Publishing Group Ltd 2004.

Finally, before leaving the section on 'rules for belonging', I want to again emphasize that while the primary rule of belonging to this group was hard core courage to endure the historical oppression, it is also important to look behind the heroics and ask *why* would people subject themselves to such harassment? What compelled them to risk losing job, family, life—if not for something 'greater than themselves'—something perhaps that felt like, 'reverence for a superhuman power', to use the dictionary definition of Divinity) worthy of worship?

Perhaps to be in the company of others who had an understanding of, acceptance of, and celebration of alternative gendering coded into sexual, and I am arguing spiritual praxis, approximated that Divinity that faith communities do feel they will 'die for', if necessary.

While I have explicated the role of the butch in facilitating a space for the acceptance of non-traditional sexual gendering in the otherwise *traditionally gendered* biological female, I want to briefly say something about the space available within butch femme for the 'stone butch'—or for the non-traditional sexual gendering in *the non-traditionally gendered* biological female.

Within this complicated, by virtue of being viewed through a necessarily dominant heterosexual lens, identity—'stone butch'—becomes pragmatic and useful viewed through the butch femme lens.

> It's hard to talk about something like giving up power without it sounding passive. I am willing to give myself over to a woman equal to her amount of wanting. I expose myself for her to see what's possible for her to love in me that's female. I want her to be open to it. I may not be doing something active with my body, but more eroticising her need that I feel in her hands as she touches me...[28]

I am suggesting that femmes created and create the space for the butch to hold and perform masculine gender. Because of this, the butch can feel 'normal' in a society wishing her to classify herself as 'abnormal'. The femme says I create space for you. Conversely, the butch creates the space for the femme to hold sexual desire in an otherwise female body traditionally gendered. Because of this, the femme can also feel normal, in a society which wishes her to feel abnormal.

> There was social pressure for butches to uphold the ideal of 'untouchability' but no equivalent ideal for femme passivity. Fems upheld the ideals of butch behaviour in order to achieve their own satisfaction. This emphasis

---

28. Amber Hollinbaugh and Cherrie Moraga, 'What We're Rollin' Around in Bed With: Sexual Silences in Feminism', in Ann Snitow, Christine Stansell and Sharon Thompson (eds.), *Powers of Desire: The Politics of Sexuality* (New York: Monthly Review Press, 1983), p. 398.

© The Continuum Publishing Group Ltd 2004.

on their own fulfilment assured fems developed sexual subjectivity, albeit differently from butches. It also balanced the power in butch femme relationships, making the pursuit of satisfaction legitimate for each partner... Butch fem relationships were gendered relationships without being fully integrated into a heterosexual system of male supremacy.[29]

Finally, in response to the stone butch, Halberstam in her new book, *Female Masculinity*, suggests that the creation of the stone butch, if viewed outside of hetero-sexist culture, is a creative and workable 'solution' to masculine gendering within the female body.

I think it is important to look again at a definition of 'pleasure', for as Halberstam suggests, a stone butch only cautions against 'unmediated' genital contact. Although some stones chose (and choose) to not orgasm with a partner, others have and do receive pleasure from their partners through a variety of sexual practises such as tribadism...'[30]

What is interesting is that one's own pleasure can 'provoke unwarranted rage not only from a gender conformist society that cannot comprehend stone butch gender or stone butch desire but also from within the dyke subculture, where the stone butch tends to be read as frigid, dysphoric, misogynist, repressed or simply pre-trans-sexual.[31]

Halberstam writes (p. 129) that 'the burden of butchness is resolved by the assumption of the stone butch identity'. I would add that the outrage against the butch may not be *merely* because she is coded by the dominant cultures as 'frigid', 'mannish', etc, but also because her praxis directly facilitates the space for the unfolding of, nurturing of, and celebration of femme desire. And historically, femme or female desire has been seen as dangerous and curtailed through historical actions such as witch burnings, rape, etc.

To create a systematic way to nurture female desire, and to create a 'worship' of that desire ('Baby, you are my church'), has not been seen as possible within history. Butch-femme created in the sexually repressed 1950s a theology of *love* with desire that was possible for not only femininely gendered women, but also masculinely gendering 'beings', in this case, women. In so doing, it presented a model for change, and therefore became a major threat to the dominant paradigm of masculine gendered repression of love, and feminine gendered repression of desire.

29. Elizabeth Lapovsky Kennedy, 'The Hidden Voice: Fems in the 1940s and 50s' (New York: Routledge, 1993), p. 25.
30. Judith Halberstam, 'Female Masculinity'; chapter 4, 'Lesbian Masculinity: Even Stone Butches Get the Blues' (Durham: Duke University Press, 1998), pp. 124-25.
31. Halberstam, 'Lesbian Masculinity', pp. 111-40.

Theological Identity of this Community

What I am suggesting is not just that butch-femme honoured the masculinely gendered woman, because, as many feminist theorists have written, the 1970s which purported to be about 'female energy' left everyone looking 'butch' and subverted female femininity's costume, and sexual passion, retaining only 'female nurturing'.

So, instead of creating a 'femininely gendered' community, they created a 'masculinely gendered' community that purported to be about losing and rejecting masculinity.

Butch femme honoured female masculinity, but also, and perhaps more radically, honoured *non-traditionally gendered* feminine women. Butch femme is one of the few spaces in all of history, that honoured as important, the feminine, the femme, especially in her sexual self.

Historically, we find evidence for femme gendered erotic pleasure being the focal point for the butch femme community.

The ability to generate and teach this body of erotic knowledge, and the passing of it from the feminine to the masculine gender, and the praxis of it, I believe may constitute the foundation of the 'theology' of this community.

Comparing Butch Femme to Male Sexuality and Other Theological Models

I have already spoken to the comparison of honouring male beauty and honouring femme beauty, present in both gay male and butch femme 'theology'.

I want to briefly state here the similarities in the creation of the gay ghetto, and the opportunities that are possible in re-visioning the 'ghetto' as a source of spiritual discovery.

> There are many ways of living as gay men. Nevertheless, I am arguing that the life style of the ghetto gays constitutes a paradigmatically determinant 'gay' way of relation to the sacred realities of gay life.
>
> ...it is only in an appreciate understanding of the ghetto's sexually promiscuous celebration of male beauty that gay theology will find its distinctive voice and power...
>
> Ghetto gays take the body so seriously that even its appearance is significant, thus perhaps the Christian idea of embodiment with a seriousness that Christian culture has never dared to.[32]

---

32. Long, 'The Sacrality of Male Beauty and Homosex', pp. 277, 280-81.

Cartier A Theology of Corporeality

This honouring of the space that is devoted to the corporeal 'theology' is also necessary within butch-femme culture, and offers the same opportunities to lesbians not involved in butch-femme — a model. Not all lesbians wish to live in butch-femme, nor should they, but the model it severs in honouring femme desire, and creating the space for butch masculinity serves to open up spaces in the lives of lesbians not committed to this lifestyle, but wanting to partake of it to a certain degree.

Certainly this was true of the middle-class, 'discreet' lesbians, who did go to the bar, if only to criticize the working-class butch-femme communities who were holding the space open for them to visit.

Kennedy and Davis write extensively about the butch need to claim space for their community, their forays into new bars, their attempts into the world and their successes and failures in claiming a corner of it. Nestle writes in the anthology *Queers in Space*, how the bar space — for her the Greenwich Village Sea Colony — gave her the opportunity, through the creation of space, to find herself and, I suggest, her 'worship tradition'.

> When I published *A Restricted Country* in 1987, I did not think in terms of queer spaces, but a basic tension in the narratives is the existence of restricted territories and my need to de-construct them into sites of lesbian freedom. Images of geography and metaphors of place came naturally to me as I tried to re-create the pre-Stonewall struggle for lesbian survival, whether concretely as a neighbourhood the Lower East Side in the 1960s — or abstractly as historical dis- enfranchisement... Silenced and policed, we congregated in allotted spaces. Borders were marked and real; vice laws, police and organized crime representatives controlled our movements into and out of our 'countries'. But what could not be controlled was what forced the creation of these spaces in the first place — our need to confront a personal destiny, to see our reflection in each other's faces and to break societal ostracism with our bodies. What could not be controlled was our desire.[33]

Since I have compared this historical community to both of these traditional religious communities in terms of praxis — that is, female agency, and the ability to hold and appreciate desire and embodiment of desire in the human flesh, I want to briefly touch here only on why these models proved insufficient for the historical community, and why a new 'theology' had to be formulated in order to hold this developing butch-femme praxis.

Because Buddhism was relatively unknown at the time of the 1950s to the Western practitioner, particularly the working-class lesbian, it is

---

33. Joan Nestle, 'Restriction and Reclamation: Lesbian Bars and Beaches of the 1950s', in Gordon Ingram, Bouthillette Brent, Marie Anne and Yolanda Retter (eds.), *Queers in Space: Communities/Public Places/Sites of Resistance* (Seattle,WA: Bay Press, 1997), p. 61.

probably sufficient to say that this model was available in terms of *access to* her, for deconstruction by the budding butch or femme.

However, Christianity was available, or rather accessible — but, simply put, not available *as* a butch or femme.

The following is emblematic of most of the response that Kennedy and Davis write about when questions of 'religious identity' come up. For the butch or femme of that period it was not possible, there *were no* standard religious models that allowed you to hold both a lesbian identity and a traditional Christian or Catholic identity.

> I was still a Catholic… I remember I had a medal around my neck, I still thought that this Catholic God was very powerful, too. I was so angry (at) what I was, and I had to accept what I was or else I would be lying…to myself and I couldn't do that. I had an idea of what was in store for me. I didn't want to face anyone, but yet I new I had to go through with this and I remember — I ripped the medal off my neck and threw it on the floor and I just thought, 'Fuck you, God, just fuck you. Just to be who I am, now look what I gotta deal with' (but)…I had to do what I was doing because I felt that it was real for me.[34]

While lesbianism has been claimed as one of traditional religion's greatest sins, it has therefore not been able to be claimed as a religious identity for many lesbians outside of, or in addition to, religious tradition. Because of the traditional church's stake in creating 'sin', I would argue that the very notion of 'religion' means homosexuality is wrong. From my interviews the general consensus appeared to be that lesbians had to live 'without religion'. It would appear that it is only the very creative lesbian who can en-vision *any sort* of God that would approve of her choice of sexual praxis.

> I can't think of butch femme as religion…because religion centres around faith in god…No…it's my lifestyle… I did go to the bars every week, and I felt like they were my family, but not necessarily 'spiritual', but just comfort. For talking, for understanding…but not spiritual…[35]

The closest that someone comes to approximating direct language of spirituality, is I agree, in the way Henking and Comstock re-vision Nestle's words simply by placing them *within* the context of a critical religious anthology — whether that is her intent or not, remains to be seen.

But, certainly artists like Chrystos, when speaking of butch femme sexual praxis, approximate very closely spiritual depths and in this case direct religious reference.

34. Kennedy and Davis, *Boots of Leather, Slippers of Gold*, p. 356.
35. 'Amazon Nan' (pseudonym), Personal Interview with Author.

© The Continuum Publishing Group Ltd 2004.

> In Her I Am
> fine dark pulsing without time...
> Slurping my tongue is a cat feather river vortex
> an angel
> We're hurtling through stars become
> here.[36]

Does 'Erotic Heritage' Make Space for Theology?
Yes. Re-visiting lesbian sexuality in the 50s allows us to re-vision our own millennium sexuality. Especially as we consider the contemporary feminist theorist dilemma that 'Mary's story' has not been told. Perhaps in re-visiting the 50s where 'Mary's story' was being lived in such an audacious way, is a path to begin to tell that story.

And I believe that in telling and exploring that story, we may begin to fashion a corporeal theology, based on the sexual praxis of butch-femme, as it was lived in the 50s.

Of course, this is a short study, and I have not been able to examine in depth the problems of violence (which were many, as in any community — working-class, upper-class, etc), but were without doubt, as has been documented in many sources, prevalent among butch femme couples — especially as their lives were under scrutiny, and not at all 'discreet'.

I do not mean to gloss over that, and suggest that the 50s were anything other than what they were. As one narrator remarked, when I questioned who she spoke of 'hanging out with':

> We hung out with prostitutes, pimps, drug dealers...because you've got to hang out with somebody...and we were felons then Don't forget that. We were criminals, ...so we hung out with criminals.[37]

But, although this was not an 'ideal community' it was also not at all a 'marginal community'. And there is serviceable material here for the contemporary lesbian to learn from, and an ability to re-frame the histories that have been written, such as Faderman's, in a new light, based on new interpretations, particularly of gender.

When a majority of one's history has been captured and trivialized — such as the witch burnings were for centuries — once that history comes to light, the reasons for its trivialization provide great lessons for contemporary societies, as well as a new window to the past.

Finally, I believe there is evidence here — in butch femme culture — from which to create a 'new' theology, based on interpretations of theol-

---

36. Chrystos, 'In Here I Am', in *In Her I Am* (Vancouver, Canada: Press Gang Publishers, 1993), p. 29.
37. Flo Fleishman, Personal Inverview with Author.

© The Continuum Publishing Group Ltd 2004.

ogy from comparison groups, and from re-visioning this period itself, without damaging the authenticity of either.

There are many different things that an individual can lay 'claim' to. Of course, one must be careful that one allows people the dignity of interpretation belonging to their time and place. However, reclaiming the 'persistent desire' of butch femme allows us a link to a true erotic heritage that may embody a truth that we desperately need.

> we have forgotten (if we ever knew) that the erotic is far more than sexuality, though it is also this. A revaluing of the erotic offers us at least two important lessons in citizenship. The first is to embrace passion. It is precisely those things which stir us most deeply that give us energy to sustain us in our work and to find joy in life. Without passion—passion …passion for music, for art, for God, for laughter, for work, for love—life becomes grim drudgery. Why would anyone care to devote him or herself to the work of justice if there is not passion in life? …the second lesson we can draw from erotic power is a reminder that we are all embodied beings. The value of erotic power calls us to revalue the physical nature of our lives and the lives of all others in society… If we want a society where people do not live in fear, we must teach future citizens that physical bodies, real human people are sacred and that avoidable human suffering of any sort is sin…Passion, sexuality, and sensuality are all physical experiences…[38]

For myself, I have found examining butch femme allows me the 'space' to acknowledge my history as 'femme', to find an erotic heritage I did not know I had, and to legitimise the need for desire in my life.

---

38. Say and Kowalewski, *Gays, Lesbians and Family Values*, p. 112.

Politics of Sexuality[1]

Pauline [Asphodel] Long

In the name of the Mother of Heaven, Mother of Earth, Creator of Life, Queen of the Sky, Queen of the Night, the Great Womb, the Throbbing Vulva, the Yoni, Most Gracious, Star Goddess, the Great Breast from which flows the milk of kindness, Goddess of Grains and Grasses, Fruitful Mother...

These are some of the titles of the Goddess remembered through the witches from earlier times. I dedicate this piece of writing in those names. They have helped me to produce the most difficult essay I have ever written.

I have tried to sort out and put together my ideas on women's values about their sexuality. Freud is said to have asked: 'What do women want?' Women know what they want. Their difficulty, which is mine, is to find words to describe, and to produce ideas acceptably. Not because we are 'silly' but because words and ideas have grown over the last 5,000 years in a patriarchal setting, and describe what men want. Every word, sentence and set of ideas is painful to write, is open to misinterpretation, certainly by men. I write here to and for women, and ask them to hear and read what I am trying to say and link it with what they find echoing in their own beings. I am going to try and write about our sexuality, its past, what happened to it in patriarchy, and what our future in a non-patriarchal world might be. I take for granted that readers will not expect me here to 'prove' that matriarchies or that goddess cultures existed.

---

1. This article was written in 1979 for the Matriarchy Study Group, London. It is included in this volume for two reasons, the first is its academic merit and the way in which it highlights that the questions are the same some 25 years later. It also shows that the way of answering them may have developed in different directions, even for the author herself, as those familiar with Asphodel's work will know. The second and more personal reason is that Asphodel is herself a grand and inspirational matriarch in the feminist theological/thealogical movement in Britain and a volume in honour of the first chair in Feminist Liberation Theology in Britain is all the richer for her inclusion.

© The Continuum Publishing Group Ltd 2004, The Tower Building, 11 York Road, London SE1 7NX and 15 East 26th Street, Suite 1703, New York, NY 10010, USA.

*The Past: Women as initiators, sexually
independent, and the concept of the whole*

Bridegroom, let me caress you,
My precious caress is sweeter than honey;
In the bed-chamber, honey-filled
Let me enjoy your goodly beauty.

This is part of a poem written for a sacred marriage in Mesopotamia about 2,000 BCE, well after the destruction of women-led cultures there, it could be thought that the woman is cajoling the man for her own purposes, or is coaxing for his. But no: such a ritual bride inherits the powers and memories of goddess cultures, where the woman takes the initiative, where her active love-making is for her own pleasure and more — for an integral understanding of wholeness. She has to be pleased and she is independent. In *Lost Gods*, John Allegro[2] describes such a sacred marriage:

> A bridal bower was erected and decorated with foliage, there the union was consummated…it is the priestess who summons the king to her embrace, and who, representing the goddess, bestows on him through their intercourse, a divine but subservient status in the more creative process.

But even more: the divine union took place between the sacred pair; but this was the occasion of love feasts for the whole community: no doubt about all sorts of sexuality — no division between single sex and hetero-, and certainly bi-sexuality. Even late records such as the Hebrew Bible and the Babylonian epics and temple documents make the situation clear. 'The Goddess Asherah was worshipped in Israel from the days of the first settlement in Canaan, the Hebrews taking over the cult of this great mother goddess from the Canaanites' says Raphael Patai in *The Hebrew Goddess*.[3]

An inscription dedicated to Ashratum (another form of this name) in the First Dynasty of Babylon (about 1,500 BCE) describes her as 'mistress of sexual vigour and rejoicing'. Becoming Ashtoreth and Astarte in the varying cultures of the Middle and Near East, and later the vengeful Anath, she is 'everywhere the great female principle' and 'the object of a sensual nature-worship, attended by many licentious rites and wild orgies'. She was the queen of heaven as well as the mother, and the opener of the womb. Upon her sexuality rested the renewing of the harvest. She is spouse and mother to the vegetation god, called many names of which Tammuz is possibly the most familiar; he becomes the Divine

---

2. John Allegro, *Lost Gods* (London: Abacus, 1953), p. 53.
3. Raphael Patai, *The Hebrew Goddess* (London: Avon Books, 1967), pp. 21-22.

King who must die, as do the green plants, and must be recalled through this communion with the earth, the womb, from which he will be reborn.

The seasonal festivals celebrating the cycle of these events were times of sexual rejoicing as well as of sacred mystery. Still remembered as 'Quarter Days' in the British Establishment calendar and in the countryside and through the earlier religions, and taken over by the Christians into religious festivals, they provide a link with women's earliest past and powers. Love, sexuality, death and rebirth reflecting the seasonal rhythms of nature were seen as an entity, and predicated always on the sexual powers of women.

John Allegro[4] suggests that the double axe, so potent a symbol throughout the ancient world, and symbol of royal power in Crete, is 'a clear fertility symbol with sexual associations. The lower edges represent the woman's opened thighs, the central shaft her vagina, and the shaft itself the penis' He suggests that there is independent philological evidence for this in all ancient languages. However, women may reflect that the reading of the penis is a male one: we can see the depths of the vagina and the cervix: we know, as Freud did not, that the opening is not a hole on its own: that it leads somewhere. Shuttle and Redgrove in *The Wise Wound*[5] give numerous examples of the whole female reproductive system being used as a sacred symbol throughout the ancient world. Perhaps the most striking suggestion is that the Tree of Knowledge and the Tree of Life are shown as the Fallopian tubes; the cervix is a vessel, the womb itself a chalice—perhaps the Holy Grail.

> I have drunk from the cymbal, I have borne the sacred vessel, I have entered the bridal chamber.

Recited by initiates into the worship of Cybele, Moon Goddess, these lines make the Mystery clear.

But, from *The Bacchae* of Euripides, Pentheus declaims:

> I hear
> Of strange and evil doings in the city,
> Of women who have left their homes to join
> Fabled mysteries…each stealing forth
> This way and that, creeps to a lawless bed;
> In pretext, holy sacrificing maenads,
> But serving Aphrodite more than Bacchus…
> Threatening the women, he includes his mother,
> 'Ino, Agave, who to Echion bore me
> Her too, Antonoe, Antaeus mother,

---

4. Allegro, *Lost Gods*, p. 63.
5. P. Shuttle and P. Redgrove, *The Wise Wound* (London: Gollancz, 1978).

And fettering them all in iron bonds,
I'll put an end to their mad wickedness'.⁶

Pentheus was destroyed by those women, but his work was taken over in full and lives on. Western literature is full of descriptions of women's 'orgies'.

They are the apologia for the holocaust of nine million women, labelled witches by European Christianity. [When this article was written, in 1979, this figure was generally accepted. Modern research indicates that the true figure is much less.]

There are two other directions I want to take before leaving the past: some thoughts about menstruation and about what has been called 'virginity'.

Menstruation: the Blessing and the Curse

Women's acceptance of their period as 'the curse' has been one of patriarchy's most successful tortures. In *Menstrual Taboos*⁷ it was recorded how menstruation was a sacred source of power, and the origin of the Sabbath: since then, Shuttle and Redgrove have documented the extraordinary relationship women's cycles have with science, religion and art, but always underground, and always denigrated. I want to mention here its direct linkage with our sexuality. Most of us experience increased sexual power just before the time of the flow, and most of us are entirely put down about it.

This links also with the concept, proposed by Esther Harding,⁸ that during menstruation and pre-menstrually we may find our inner life, and withdraw from a patriarchal world. The conflicts and 'bitchiness' so well-documented by Dr Katerina Dalton are likely because of the inability of our inner selves to have any possibility of recognition; while experimenting for ecstasy just at the time of the flow has not apparently been on anybody's agenda (although perhaps lesbians could have something to say about this). There is immense potential in coming to terms with our cycle; certainly some of the Eastern religions have taken it over, and have subverted Kundalini and serpent power to male use. It is time that we take it back to ourselves, where it belongs.

There is another aspect: I believe that our monthly cycles, related timewise as they always were to the moon's movements, were the foundation of mathematical calculation. I believe that the counting up of menstrual

---

6.   Euripides, *The Bacchae* (London: Dent, 1951).
7.   Matriarchy Study Group, London, 1978.
8.   Esther Harding, *The Way of All Women* (London: Rider, 1971).

rhythms led to the building of giant megalithic science observatories, and provide us with truly not concrete, but stone, examples of the relationship of the sexual with the intellectual, and are in themselves the expression of the totality of women's sexual life. The possible relationship of menstruation to such gigantic intellectual and mechanical advance is only now becoming a matter of study. It is no coincidence that male power which took over the intellect found it so necessary to degrade an aspect of it so closely connected with women's sexuality.

Virgins and Prostitutes

Patriarchal writers speak contemptuously of 'temple harlots' throughout the early records. At the same time, the Mother of Jesus was, and is revered as 'virgin'. They have also insisted that virginity meant without knowledge of or experience of sexual intercourse. Virgins were pure, even holy. Virgins were also the 'sacred vessel', 'uncontaminated', which men could violate for their own purposes, and proceed to own and enslave totally for life.

There is ample evidence that temple harlots are also temple virgins. That is, they are the wives of the sacred kings, and priestesses of the Goddess, putting their sexuality at the service of the community for its benefit. The meaning of 'virgin', says Esther Harding (and others) was 'one in herself', 'not married', 'sexually independent'. Harding says: 'The male worshipper sought for union with the Goddess...the woman pledged to a religious life would not enter into secular marriage...even women not so pledged were required to give themselves once in their lifetime in the temple'.[9] Herodotus called it 'the worst Babylonian custom'. But he commented: 'after intercourse she made herself holy'. Children born of these unions were children of the temple and of the community: often they were called 'the sons of God'. All children conceived by the temple virgins were the offspring of the sacred king, the divine son/lover of the Goddess.

Raphael Patai refers to the quedeshim, male sacred prostitutes, and suggests their function 'in rites of imitative magic, was to ensure fruitfulness in nature, the coming of the autumn rains, the growth of the crops'.[10]

One more look at our past, to lead us into the present — and one very much based on our 'cultural heritage'.

The Song of Solomon, written about 200 BCE and included in the Old Testament, is an overt description of sexuality and as such an embarrass-

---

9. Harding *The Way of All Women*, p. 75.
10. Patai, *The Hebrew Goddess*, p. 23.

ment to the establishment. It need not be. In fact, it is one of our first and most easily available records of our put-down sexually.

Woman is cast as a sex object, and her natural feelings of love are disdained:

> My beloved put his hand by the hole ('of the door', added by the translator) and my bowels were moved for him. I rose up to open up to my beloved... I opened to my beloved, but my beloved had withdrawn himself and was gone... I sought him but could not find him. I called him but he gave me no answer. The watchmen that went about the city found me. They smote me, they wounded me, the keepers of the wall took away my veil from me [euphemism for rape] (Song 5.4-7).

But the man is just not with her: we sense the difference in his love talk:

> How fair is my sister, my spouse...thou hast ravished my heart with one of thine eyes...how much better is thy love than wine, and the smell of thine ointment than all spices... a garden enclosed is my sister, a spring shut up, a fountain sealed (Song 4.10).

This brings us up through 2,000 years to:

The Present

For all that time, we have been a garden enclosed, a spring shut up, a fountain sealed. How this horror happened cannot be chronicled here. A lamentation written after the destruction of the Moon City of Ur of the Chaldees is addressed to the Goddess—and describes our situation to this very day.

> Oh Queen, how can you stay alive
> After your city has been destroyed, how can you exist
> Your righteous house which has been given over to the pickaxe and you no longer inhabit it,
> Your people have been led to the slaughter and you are no longer their Queen ('The Lament of Or').[11]

Did we stay alive? Have we been mutated by oppression? Or have we fought an underground resistance, hidden even from ourselves and our sisters. For all of us who have gone down to the grave in grief and silence as well as in the utmost horror of rape and violence, there has, has there not, been a memory of inner integrity, of our sexuality—always disappointed—that we know is right. And linked with this our natural rhythm and its consequences.

---

11. 'The Lament of Or', in Thorkild Jacobsen, *The Harps that Once* (New Haven, CT: Yale University Press, 1987), pp. 463-69.

Patriarchy and Women's Sexuality

But, talking about natural rhythms gets us nowhere without getting down to our lives under patriarchy and its relationship to our sexuality.

Patriarchy, however and whenever it happened, took women out of the community and put them to slave labour for a particular man who in return kept them alive in order to serve his needs and those of 'his' children. This had an immediate economic effect: the reversal of women's power and independence in their own right, to become the creatures of particular men. It must always be remembered that in the ancient world, women and children formed part of the economic set-up; they supported themselves and each other through their labour; whether the male contribution was equal or not is a matter for investigation. It has been shown that as far back as the hunter-gatherers, women's labour brought in up to 80 per cent of the food supplies on a regular basis. The *Mabinogion* chronicles the times of the ancient Celts before marriage subdued women showing them as strong and independent; from the *Mabinogion*, quoted in *Island of the Mighty* by Evangeline Walton.[12]

> In my youth, men and women desired each other and were joined, and parted when desire was over-past. Nor was there argument or curiosity or lewd speculation regarding the origins of children, for these were the gifts with which the high gods blessed women, we had no disrespect for women in those days. Now all in Gwyned know that Math and Don were born of the same mother, and the women still live who saw Don give birth to Gwydion. Our royal house is above a doubt. When you have seen them with your eyes, you know.[13]

Jean Markale in *Women of the Celts*[14] shows they were economically independent and equal; they were even able to take back their marriage dowries in the event of divorce, they owned property, and carried prominent social prestige. With the coming of patriarchal power, women's economic situation plummeted. The economics are not difficult. For several thousand years men have owned women's bodies, their labour power, and claimed access to their sexuality on a twenty-four-hour-a-day lifelong basis, from a slave master standpoint and with the women expected to comply, with no rights whatsoever. Men's first economic power has been over women; they live on the labour of the woman, and cannot take their own part in economic society without the base structure of women's slavery. Added to this, their role as money-earner has

---

12. Evangeline Walton, *Island of the Mighty* (New York: Ballentine, 1970).
13. Walton, *Island of the Mighty*, p. 21.
14. Jean Markale, *Women of the Celts* (London: Cremonesi, 1975), pp. 21-30.

given them sexual power. What woman has not had to 'coax' sexually; what woman knows nothing about the fear of rejection or disapproval of the 'master'; what woman has not put her own needs down in bed? What woman has not felt that she has no real rights at all to her sexuality, that she is abnormal, that there is no point in even trying? What woman has not been left sexually aroused, and given no care? Even today, in so-called 'liberated' circles, if women have not come to orgasm by the time the man is 'tired', she can be expected to masturbate, or to use a vibrator. What woman has not often faked an orgasm just to get the whole thing over, or to please the master, or to get some sleep before the children wake?

More: what woman has not become terrified if her period is late, if she is pregnant. Where are her hard won rights under patriarchy? Where is her career, her scholarship, her job, her interests, her independence? All in the control of a single man, to whom she has to yield her soul's light as well as her body's.

It seems silly to write about this, because we all know it, and how for the last hundred years or so women have won some few social and economic rights in the Western world soon abrogated with pregnancy. Men have come to expect women's dependence as a normal state of affairs and usually resent any divergence, although they grumble about their roles as 'breadwinner' etc. But a woman, when pregnant, has the choice of violating her body or accepting longterm imprisonment with hard labour and no parole. Where are our natural rhythms now? Gone underground.

A sociological survey in 1978, called 'Social Origins of Depression', found women's depression is brought about by 'severe life events'. Women most vulnerable to depression were those who had three or more children under 14 living at home; said the researchers: 'Lack of an outside job lowers resistance to depression'. The risk is practically halved when a woman has a job (even doing the treble work of the job, of home, and the husband). The researchers suggest that common to all the depression factors in women is a 'lack of self esteem'. Wife- and Motherhood are the cause of this: a 'job', however trivial, gives a woman a sense of worth in society — as well as a wage for herself making her into an object of 'value'.

When we become mothers, it looks for a short time as if we can find some inner independence, but our work is always not just under-valued, but non-valued. Eventually our sons grow up to call us an old boot; and our daughters to revile us. Motherhood is the means whereby we are divested of any kind of independence and made totally subject; but expected to continue to make our major contribution to society, with no help, no support, no recognition.

© The Continuum Publishing Group Ltd 2004.

Society underpins our guilt always; everything is always our fault. If we escape from the man and become 'single parents' usually our situation is execrable; privatisation of our predicament induces guilt of the worst sort—quite irrelevant, but there nonetheless; often giving our children powers of tyranny that distort their lives as well as ours; and where men are concerned, puts us in the unenviable position of having to try to 'conform' to their ideas of sexuality, keeping the children out of the way. There is nothing for us there at all. Even in modern 'alternative' frameworks, there is little or no acceptance of children as being of the community; always when the crunch comes, it is a case of 'It's your child, deal with it yourself'.

Dorothy Dinnerstein, in her monumental *The Rocking of the Cradle and the Ruling of the World*,[15] post-dates the Freudian position on the mother. She links equality of child care between women and men as the means of freeing ourselves sexually from the misconceptions brought about by women's necessity in patriarchy to be the single source of power in children's lives. The mother becomes the ogre and the 'witch' if she withholds anything; the son grows up with a drive to get the magical provider under his control; the daughter is torn between her need for male-style independence and her association with her mother; and further, she looks for 'mothering' in the man—he is the one, surely, to nurture her, support her, care for her: what pain, what disappointment. Distorted sexual needs are born, suggests Dinnerstein, of this patriarchal relationship. Only when the 'first parent' is equally female and male can a truer appreciation of our sexuality become open to us, she believes.

Patriarchy and Sexuality

The position that patriarchy has achieved for women's sexuality today can adequately be summed up by a look at an issue of Women's International Network News (WIN) published in the USA (1978). Starting with female circumcision still taking place in 26 countries, WIN quotes from an 'International Year of the Child' report: Besides the psychological aspects, the effects of this genital excision results in severe health hazards both at the time of the operation and during the childbearing years. WIN highlights Mwalimu Julius Nyerere's speech inaugurating International Women's Year 1975. The speech singled out the customs of dowry and polygamy as incompatible with Africa's cardinal struggle for the attainment and maintenance of human dignity. Female circumcision, correctly

---

15. Dorothy Dinnerstein, *The Rocking of the Cradle and the Ruling of the World* (London, Souvenir Press, 1978), pp. 2-9.

known as clitoridectomy, is the removal of the clitoris—the female sex organ. Another form of oppression which women are subjected to, and perhaps the cruellest, is infibulation. This is the closing up of the labia of a girl to ensure her virginity. The labia (lips of the vagina) are sewn shut at puberty and opened forcibly at marriage…this custom reduces woman to a mere tool for the man's pleasure, with no rights over her own body. It is a common belief among the old women—a belief usually encouraged by midwives who make their living from these antiquated practices —that unless the introitus is tightened as much as possible by circumcision, the girl cannot be pleasing to a man. That the other women encourage this practice is of course one of the saddest aspects of patriarchal conditioning.[16]

Other sections of WIN deal with Women and Violence,[17] listing family violence, wife battering and rape. Oppressions of women in the environment, in the media, in the home, divorce in the Moslem world are all chronicled. Who of us does not know of the indignity of walking in a street, sitting in a train, sitting on a park bench? We are unable to claim the basic human right of breathing fresh air or walking in the city. This is everywhere, in every so-called 'civilised' place in the world. All of us know the sexual put-downs; all of us have had our sexual organs referred to as degraded parts of the human system; all of us know the fear of rape. All the put-down is something to do with our sexuality: and man's fear of it. We have been made into sex objects, made 'dirty', we 'appeal to the lower side of man's nature'. We are a nothing, a no-one.

In the name of the Mother, the Despised, the Disdained, the Derided, the Raped, the Scorned, the Unenvied, the Neglected, the One of No Account.

I am attacked by a woman, now pregnant, who has been a strong activist in politics and resents the current heaviness and restriction of her life and fears for what is to come. She says she envies me my freedom (I am past child bearing now) and she hates the 'wallowing in so-called femininity' that she believes the Goddess followers and matriarchal women advocate. She says: 'You are so ambivalent, you praise matriarchy, but you know what motherhood's like. It's like death'. She talks

---

16. 25 years later this is still carried out and indeed the British government makes provision for it to occur here if it is shown to be 'necessary' due to cultural or psychological needs.

17. Family violence is increasing and sociologists suggest that as masculinity remains in crisis levels of violence to women will rise still higher. One woman a week is killed in the home in Britain, the figure is 12 per week in the USA. One in four women can expect to be raped in Britain.

about her cruel need to depend on the child's father, and she adds: 'Anyhow, you are not a true feminist because you go with men'.[18] What she says raises crucial questions for me.

The Matriarchy Study Group in its Manifesto suggests different types of support for mothers and children in a communal and co-operative setting. In such circumstances, motherhood need not be like death, it may come into its own, as a pleasure and a delight.[19]

I want to talk about her cry: you are not a true feminist because you go with men.

Patriarchy at the Immediate Present

Beatrix Campbell presented a history of women's sexuality since 1968, in a dynamic lecture launching Feminist Review.[20] She showed how the 1968 liberation movement was liberation for men; exploitation of a new sort of woman.[21] Free sex on men's terms became pressure for unlimited sexual availability on women; news about women's possibility of multiple orgasm provided the need for this to be obtained at every meeting: if the man was unable to bring the woman to this (or to orgasm at all) it then became her duty to comfort him, to reassure him, and to assume the mother role. Her needs were seen as entirely complementary to his; she became an honorary man—except in 'revolutionary' terms. There, he was still the boss (and remains so). Men were disinclined to view women's oppression as other than their own. Sexual oppression was seen in traditional class terms. They were not willing to see it as the primal oppression which it is.

Here I want, personally, to state what I call 'Pauline's [Asphodel's] Law'. This is: Women and Men are Everywhere Oppressed, but wherever the man is oppressed, the woman is doubly or trebly oppressed. Her basic oppression starts, continues and never ends in bed.

Back to Bea Campbell: men's behaviour and women's disappointment at the failure of the freedom revolution led them, she suggests, to the political Lesbian alternative. Now women found they were able to throw off male oppression completely, and to relate solely to each other, and felt strong enough to come out and do so. But, in spite of the close and loving relationships, where, she asked, were the supportive frameworks,

18. This was a question much debated in the 1960s and 1970s.
19. Sadly 25 years later the government still likes to blame mothers, particularly single mothers, and to make living conditions difficult by the restrictions on benefit.
20. Beatrix Campbell, 'Women's Sexuality' (unpublished lecture, October 1978).
21. Sheila Jeffreys has written about this in recent years, see for example, *Anticlimax: A Feminist Perspective on the Sexual Revolution* (London: The Women's Press, 1990).

the houses, the creches, the financial networks for mothers and children? So far everything was seen in privatised terms—though part of the essential framework of women's politics. But the loudest silence, she claimed, had been from the heterosexual women. Where were they, what had they to say, were women to be defeated again?

The Future

Changing consciousness is immensely painful and difficult. We women have to get out of our patriarchal thinking and responding; we have to sick up the poison we have ingested since birth. Researching our past puts confidence and strength into us, and particularly into our sexuality, which at the same time extends even to spiritual as well as to physical liberation. But there is more than that.

Anger and Justice

We have to get in touch with our anger. Recalling the past leads us to a new vision of the future. But this future is held back by men. Reflecting in their sexual life with us their depersonalisation, their alienation from life, their emotional shiftlessness and irresponsibility, their lack of care and selfishness which so often leads us to madness and suicide. No longer.

In the name of Kali the Destroyer, the Avenger, the Cleanser, in the name of Maeve and the Morrigan, in the name of the Holder of the Scales of Justice.

We women have to call upon our anger. We have to reach for it and let it loose. Until our anger boils over, we will not be free people. So often we bury it, we 'forgive', we turn it into pain, acceptably weep, wash up and smile again. No longer. There can be no future for us until we uncover the spring which is now a volcano, and let it go where it has to. We have to seek justice.

Revolution? Puny men have not started: all they achieve is an ecstasy of violence followed by punitive power. When we reach our anger and when they stand and face it and accept it, understanding that whatever comes they have deserved, then there might just be a future for our heterosexuality, even for the human race.

Their patriarchal control of nature has run it on to a destruction course, there is almost no time left to reverse this. Their oppression of us has created a depersonalised world, they rape nature as they rape us, they demand continual replenishment of their own resources from ours. No longer.

Without our anger, nothing will change. We have no longer to be patient, to cope, to be sympathetic, to uphold their sky.

Men are less whole than we are, less able to heal themselves, unable to avoid venting their toxic distortions on us. I don't know if they will ever become whole people, or even want to do so. Certainly they will not, until they face their oppressive power and its consequences, and our anger and its consequences. I see men today, aware of something of the past, now trying to learn caring mechanisms and taking responsibility for children. I see gay men learning and helping other men to learn about and nourish their emotions. I see men going into brotherhood groups to seek to understand their feelings better. Very well. But I see no men coming to grips with their oppression of women. They back away continually, and will not come to judgment. I see no future for our heterosexuality unless they can take this step forward. There is a historic necessity being forced on them. The wretched whom they have trodden into the earth for so long are rising up and calling for accounts to be taken.

If men are not able to understand this and adapt to the changes needed, then they will have run themselves into an evolutionary blind alley and eventually become extinct. If men ask themselves why they should bother to change themselves and confront women's anger; why even, they should become 'persons' rather than patriarchs, why they should give up their privileged life on slave labour, they might reflect on this: already patriarchal ways of living in the Western world have shortened their lifespan significantly compared with women's; soon, if they persist in their dinosaur- tyrannosaur-like behaviour, there will be no use for them whatever in the world, and they will go to the scrap heap.

Gynandry – Beyond Androgyny

But I don't think this is a necessary or a welcome path. An article by Andrea Dworkin in *Peace News* said:

> There are two emerging feminist erotic models – Lesbianism and Androgyny. Lesbianism is the celebration of womanhood, the core erotic act in an emerging woman's culture. Androgyny has to do with the obliteration of gender distinctions and sex roles and ultimately of gender itself.[22]

Yes. But I am going to call androgyny something else, and hope it will be something else. This is gynandry.

Gynandry is more than androgyny. It is not a case of the obliteration of gender distinctions based on patriarchal conditioning. It might encour-

---

22. Andrea Dworkin, 'Feminism and the Radical Left', *Peace News* (December, 1978).

age personal distinctiveness and bring gender differences to ecstasy. It may even create new genders. Implicit in it is personhood for every person: each person will take part in communal care of all, and of each other. While women need not forego the pleasures of femaleness and mothering, they will allow motherhood to other sexes too. There will be new technology which will bring the choice of having children in or out of the body.

We have to face this future with great care: in a person-run world, with women in command of what happens to them, such technology can relieve them of the slavery and drudgery associated with children and release the total joy that is so often stifled. Women who do not want to use their bodies for this purpose need not: those who do will have the choice of doing so without penalty. But in a patriarchal context, such technology is a vicious threat: more control of women's bodies by men, and even genetic engineering to create supermonsters in their own image. Our matriarchal values are needed more urgently here than at any other point: caring and nurturing, freedom and loving have to be the core of such technology, otherwise it is true death to us all. At the heart of such caring is communal support for those who need it, freedom to pursue our whole lives, and a complete destruction of patriarchy. I look at Marge Piercy's *Woman at the Edge of Time* and Naomi Mitchison's *Memoirs of a Spacewoman* for ideal pictures of what this situation could be like.

And now for some points about our sexuality now and in the future.

Clitoral and Vaginal Orgasm

I am doubtful about the significance of the physical gap between the clitoris and the vagina. I wonder (with Elaine Morgan[23]) whether there is a Natural Selection factor. Why should penetration of the penis into the vagina not give similar satisfaction to the woman as to the man? Some believe this can be achieved through sexual dexterity and through learning in children's early play how to please oneself and others. But I go further.

Have women been physically neglected for so long that our body geography has changed? Statuettes of Cretan women in the Heraklion Museum show them with clitoris much more enlarged than is usual today. Our capacity for multi-orgasm is much under-used. Can our clitorises have shrunk through lack of use? If so, how long and how much activity will it take to get them right again?

---

23. Elaine Morgan, *Descent of the Woman* (London: Souvenir Press, 1972).

Another suggestion: Is our bodily make-up such that we need not one, but several partners? Sherfey in her *Nature and Evolution of Female Sexuality*[24] thought that we did, and that society put us down in order to create and retain 'law and order'. Suppose we are made so that when one partner gets tired, another takes over; or should we in fact enjoy our sexuality in common, single sex, bisexually, always, sometimes, not at all, or only at seasonal festivals?

More or Less Sex?

Paula Tree, in her *Liberating Sexuality*,[25] a book of real love and care, suggests that in a future where people are more tender and caring of each other the needs of our sexuality would be lessened. In fact, instead of having sex without love, we might have love without sex. This could be a releasing thought, but I don't go the whole way with it. With the message of the past before us I think we could get back to integrating our sexuality with spirituality. Sexuality will not just yield a pleasant pastime, but become a matter of sacred reverence and put us in touch with our wholeness. It will become more, not less important.

Kundalini and Serpent Power

As our sexual slavery disappears, we might relearn some of the older knowledge. It is not possible to deal here with the concept of Serpent Power, now taken over by male devotees. The serpent, symbol always of women's wisdom, immortality and totality, stretches from our womb to our nipples, coiled round the tree of life inside us. Control of it must come back to us, and we may, if we choose, only then share it with male partners.

Conclusion

I find it necessary to repeat an all-important point made in this article. For gynandry to be more than a pious hope, it must have a social and economic framework. We have to conjecture a new kind of matriarchal situation on the basis of community responsibility. If anyone reading this, thinks such matters have nothing to do with her sexuality, let her imagine, when next fucking, how she would feel if that world were already in being.

24. Mary Jane Sherfey, *Nature and Evolution of Female Sexuality* (London: Vintage Books, 1976).
25. Paula Tree, *Liberating Sexuality* (London: Penguin Books, 1978).

© The Continuum Publishing Group Ltd 2004.

Gynandry assumes the adulthood of humankind. Gender may become irrelevant and whether it does so also becomes irrelevant. The more important questions of who has the power, who is the community, are touched upon (as far as we are able) in our Manifesto. (There is more work to be done here.) I believe that person-hood is connected with nurturing, but that no longer do we women have to nurture men. I repeat: we have nurtured so much that we now must have retribution, and we must have restitution. We cry out for justice, and we will obtain justice.

Am I not a true feminist because I go with men? This accusation caused me a lot of heart-searching and I have come to the conclusion that I can't answer it. But I want to say something important for me. For all the life-long disappointments (and they never stop), and the agony, I do not want to deny the joy that has happened to me. This joy has always been bound up with the natural world, the sea, the dark flowing river with flocks of birds overhead. This has been with a man. This joy has led to the knowledge of the concept of the Goddess and to my re-entering and understanding my magic powers and possibilities, to a knowledge of death and of re-birth.

To women who want to love men, to women who bear sons, women who are now sitting crying, disappointed, agonised, despairing: with you I weep constantly, with you I reach for my anger, with you I fight on, with you I dedicated myself again—In the Name of the Mother.[26]

---

26. I would like to acknowledge the support of the women from the Matriarchy Study Group—Lynn who posed the question; Pauline who when I cried out in desperation 'I can't go forward, I can't go back' said 'Well get into it then'. In this she reminded me of the midwife at the birth of my second child, I said 'I'm stuck, I can't go on' and she responded 'What is your alternative?' I am grateful to her too. Thanks to Helen who said it is alright to not always know the answers, it is OK to say you are confused and to Dot who, as always, helped me find strength.

© The Continuum Publishing Group Ltd 2004.

Witches and Words

Naomi R. Goldenberg

I ask you to think about two quotations dating back to the 1970s. The first is a translation from Xaviére Gauthier's opening statement for a literary review dedicated to exploring women's creativity. The publication was called 'Sorcires' and the statement is appropriately titled 'Pourquoi Sorcières?':

> Why witches? Because witches sing. Can I hear this singing? It is the sound of another voice. They tried to make us believe that women did not know how to speak or write; that they were stutterers or mutes. That is because they tried to make women speak straightforwardly, logically, geometrically, in strict conformity. In reality, they croon lullabies, they howl, they gasp, they babble, they shout, they sigh. They are silent and even their silence can be heard.[1]

The second is just three lines from US feminist Robin Morgan's oft-cited work titled *Monster*:

> And I will speak less and less to you
> And more and more in crazy gibberish you cannot understand:
> witches' incantations, poetry, old women's mutterings...[2]

Does it seem odd that Xaviére Gauthier, author and editor, and Robin Morgan, poet, should invoke the image of witches speaking in eccentric, often scorned genres of language in order to further their goal of enhancing women's authority and promoting feminist reforms? I don't think very many of us find it odd at all. I think we understand that through the metaphor of witches' speech Gauthier and Morgan are calling on the world to pay attention to the new words they want to say — to the words that will be sufficiently deep — in both a psychological and collective sense — that they will sound intoxicating, transformative, crazy, scary and, above all, powerful.

---

1. Xaviére Gauthier, 'Pourquoi Sorcières?', in Elaine Marks and Isabelle de Courtivron (eds.), *New French Feminisms: An Anthology* (New York: Schoken Books, 1980), p. 199.
2. Robin Morgan, *Monster* (New York: Vintage Books, 1972), p. 85.

© The Continuum Publishing Group Ltd 2004, The Tower Building, 11 York Road, London SE1 7NX and 15 East 26th Street, Suite 1703, New York, NY 10010, USA.

Using witchy words as magic words, that is, as words to make things happen, was not an uncommon practice in 1970s feminism. For example, a group of New York activists who staged acts of political theatre, such as hexing bridal fairs, named themselves with the acronym W.I.T.C.H., standing for the Women's International Terrorist Conspiracy from Hell. This creative, playful group successfully garnered much attention from the media and breathed some life into left-wing politics. The initials were adopted by other 'covens' with more specific goals such as 'Women Inspired to Commit Herstory' or 'Women Incensed at Telephone Company Harassment'.

I can testify to the ability of witchy words to work magic. In 1977, I was teaching in a besieged Department of Religion at Central Michigan University in Mt. Pleasant, Michigan. We were a group of seven—three of whom were on temporary contracts because enrollment was down. We lived in fear of the university's statistician who was continually counting our students with the objective of firing one of us should the number dip. Having recently met both Z Budapest and Starhawk, I thought I'd introduce a course inspired by their work. I called it 'Witchcraft, Magic and Occult Phenomena'. Almost immediately, 200 students signed up. Our enrolment problem was solved and all our jobs were safe.

For several years, I pursued my interest in the Craft—in both its ancient and contemporary forms. I helped bring both Z and Starhawk to meetings of the American Academy of Religion so that more scholars could become familiar with the new feminist revival of the Old Religion. I remember that my feminist sisters gladly ceded me the honor of introducing Z since they worried that being too closely associated with witchcraft might not enhance their academic careers. As a Jewish atheist in the pious, and largely Christian field of religious studies, I already felt marginalized and was not concerned about further censure. Putting the feminist witches in contact with the feminist scholars was a fine move: Z and Starhawk signed book contracts and produced volumes which, to my delight, have been fixtures on the syllabi of Women and Religion classes for nearly two decades.[3]

I will explain why I, an inveterate atheist, find witchcraft so interesting and significant. I can not be a witch in an orthodox sense since I can not

---

3. For example, Z. Budapest, *The Holy Book of Women's Mysteries* (Oakland: Wingbow Press, 1986); and *The Grandmother of Time: A Woman's Book of Celebrations, Spells and sacred Objects for Every Month of the Year* (San Francisco: Harper & Row, 1989. Also Starhawk, *The Spiral Dance: The Rebirth of the Religion of the Great Goddess* (New York: Harper & Row, 1979); and *Truth or Dare: Encounters with Power, Authority and Mystery* (San Francisco: HarperSanFrancisco, 1987).

entertain belief in any deity whatever qualities of gender or limitations are imputed to her, it or him. To me, all religions are important fictions, a word derived from the Latin verb *facere*, to make. We make religions and we live and die within their narratives and designated behaviors. This makes the study of religions inseparable from the study of culture.[4]

Witchcraft attracts me because it is rife with magical discourse that encourages us to play with fire. We all recognize magic words when we hear them, and witchy words have magic. Aleister Crowley, a skilled magician of deservedly ill-repute, once defined magic as 'the Science and Art of causing Change to occur in conformity with Will'.[5] In a very general way, the word witch has magic in the sense of Crowley's definition because it brings to mind what every patriarchal institution shuts out: namely, fantasies of maternal, sexual power in all of its complicated, messy, marvelous manifestations.

Discursive, institutionalized systems connected to organized religions, governments, universities, and armies are built around imagery that idealizes male adulthood such as lines of paternal descent, male ritual gatherings and processions, and phallic attributes of power. Witches embody other psychological and social forces. The word witch can conjure female carnality, deep emotion, imaginings that border on madness, the playfulness and vulnerability of infancy and old age, the perpetual birth and decay of the natural world. Witches thus are well-positioned to make institutions nervous by calling attention to that which a dominant patriarchal order must occlude.

Mention of witches' wails and incantations, the mutterings of crones, their rhymes, their prophecies, their so-called gibberish summons up specters and visions of suppressed portions of minds, histories and desires. Ancient grievances and exclusions are referenced in these forms of language as are human limits and longings. Because witchy words can touch us so deeply, they have the power to disrupt ordinary speech and thus disturb business as usual. They wield creative leverage and make space for something new to happen—something other than the routinized performance of patriarchal grandiosity.

Witchy creativity has been evident in both contemporary religious movements and the field of religious studies for the last two decades. Myriad groups across North America meet to perform rituals and to honor the goddess in idiosyncratic ways. A recent, excellent study of

---

4. I am attracted to the argument that religious studies ought to be incorporated into cultural studies. See for example, Timothy Fitzgerald, *The Ideology of Religious Studies* (New York: Oxford University Press, 2000).

5. Aleister Crowley, *Magick in Theory and Practice* (New York: Castle Books, 1968), p. xii.

such groups in Canada observes that practitioners of the Craft prefer rites and behaviors that are 'elective rather than prescribed'. Encouraging religious innovations that permit individuals to speak about an 'unmediated connection with the divine' thus seems to be one of the main attractions of neo-paganism.[6]

Scholars and theologians have joined practitioners in helping to found a flourishing movement and discourse that promotes the worship of female divinities. With precision and clarity, Melissa Raphael traces the complex lines of discussion and debate which characterize the phenomenon in her book *Introducing Thealogy*.[7] In the chapter titled 'Feminist Witchcraft', Raphael points to a development that I have noted with some ambivalence: namely, that witchcraft is turning into a credible spiritual option for both congregants and religious theorists. The following quotation from rabbi and anthropologist Howard Eilberg-Schwartz concludes Raphael's chapter:

> The witch is no longer an 'other' that helps by way of negation to define who we are. Nor is the witch an entity against whom we can and must collectively unite. On the contrary, witches are now recognizable and respectable members of our society with whom we share a great many common interests and values.[8]

The domestication of the witch and the routinization of goddess talk affects me with a perverse sense of disappointment. I worry that one of my favorite discursive methods for problematizing regimens of religious thought is losing its edge. I am now looking in other places to find material. I find myself interested in queering the concept of religion. I would like to participate in discussions that subject the term 'religion' to radical interrogation similar to that which Judith Butler practices in regard to the concept of gender.[9] However, my earlier interest in witchcraft is not incompatible with this project. For me, an important use of the Craft has been as a deconstructive tool to loosen the fabric of traditional religious thought. By celebrating both women and the natural world, the Craft sets itself up as both competitor with, and critic of, mainstream religions.

---

6. Sian Lee MacDonald Reid, 'Disorganised Religion: An Exploration of the Neopagan Craft in Canada' (Unpublished Doctoral Thesis, Carleton University, Ontario, 2001).

7. Melissa Raphael, *Introducing Thealogy: Discourse on the Goddess* (Sheffield: Sheffield Academic Press, 1999).

8. Howard Eilberg-Schwartz, 'Witches of the West: Neopaganism and Goddess Worship as Enlightenment Religions', in *Journal of Feminist Studies in Religion* (1989), pp. 77-95 as cited by Raphael, *Introducing Thealogy*, p. 156.

9. Judith Butler, Bodies That Matter: On the Discursive Limits of Sex (New York: Routledge, 1993).

I worry that if attending to goddesses imitates traditional religious formulations, the Craft will simply become 'another of the same', that is, a variant of standard theological ideologies regarding an exalted deity.[10] I might have to look elsewhere for the refreshing iconoclasm conjured by 'crazy gibberish and incantations'.

Nevertheless, lately, I have come to understand that thealogy and witchcraft are a long way from losing their radical efficacy. Although I worry about whether or not success will spoil the Craft, others fear that the goddess is posing a serious threat to the hegemony of traditional religious thought. Once again, the goddess is under attack. This time her most potent detractors are to be found in the ranks of the sisterhood. Those feminist theorists and theologians among us who know the value of witchiness ought to speak up.

Prominent among goddess critics is Cynthia Eller in her book *The Myth of Matriarchal Prehistory: Why an Invented Past Won't Give Women a Future*.[11] Eller argues that because evidence for a glorious matriarchal past is slim, women are wrong to find inspiration for personal and social change by studying the female forms and figures depicted in ancient artifacts and architecture. Her polemical purpose requires her to minimize what seems to me to be the obvious presence of female symbolism in Paleolithic art. She doubts that allusions to vulvas and other parts of female anatomy could possibly be abundant in prehistoric carvings and sculpture. After all, she writes, these images, 'are very simple to draw... they may mean nothing, prehistoric doodles...'[12]

I agree that Eller has made a useful contribution to scholarship by pointing out that feminist claims about societies of the deep past are based on conjecture. What she neglects to consider, however, is that all claims about Paleolithic and Neolithic worlds are highly uncertain. For decades, archaeologists have been imagining what they believe might have been true about prehistoric societies. Often, these hypotheses reflect our present patriarchal order and thus derive a certain credibility by depicting an ancient version of our contemporary religious practices. I have written elsewhere to describe a process whereby a flimsy archaeological interpretation can appear plausible to an audience simply because it reiterates expected conventions.[13]

---

10. S.N. Balagangadhara, in *The Heathen in His Blindness: Asia the West and the Dynamic of Religion* (Leiden: E.J. Brill, 1994).

11. Cynthia Eller, *The Myth of Matriarchal Prehistory: Why an Invented Past Won't Give Women a Future* (Boston: Beacon Press, 2000).

12. Eller, *The Myth of Matriarchal Prehistory*, p. 120.

13. Naomi Goldenberg, 'Marija Gimbutas and the King's Archeologist', in *Journal of Feminist Studies in Religion* 12.2 (1996), pp. 67-72.

What I find important about feminist thought about Paleolithic history is not its historical accuracy, since that can never be established conclusively. I am interested in the ways women are using imagination about the deep past to fuel their political goals in the present. If I could influence the terms of this discourse, I would advise feminist matriarchalists to portray themselves more explicitly as poets and visionaries and less as empiricists. All religions interpret history to serve their aspirations. Feminist thealogy could demonstrate a high level of honesty and sophistication by freely admitting the speculative nature and inspirational objectives of its historical reconstructions.

Another prominent opponent of witchcraft and thealogy is Rosemary Ruether. In early March 2002, I attended two of Ruether's lectures at a conference in Ottawa called 'Healing the Earth: A Challenge for Feminism and Theology'.[14] Certain themes in these talks deserve critique. Although I much appreciate the valuable and copious work that Ruether has done for the field of women and religion and applaud the support she continues to provide for women and minorities in scholarship and ministry, I think it important to call attention to that small portion of her work which would, in my opinion, limit the scope and reach of feminist theory.

Ruether's opposition to what I am calling witchiness is sometimes inconsistent. In her lectures and published work, she will occasionally compliment thealogians and refer to them as friends, as she did once or twice on the occasion I am describing. This ambivalence is a hopeful sign that indicates a willingness on Ruether's part to make space for witchy discourse. With the goal of encouraging discussion of issues related to the scope and range of feminist theory, I will point out aspects of Ruether's work that I find restrictive.

Ruether appears to maintain that goddess religions do not provide a good basis for ethical behavior. Melissa Raphael has done a fine job of relating some of the history behind Ruether's past formulations of this assertion as well as the reasoned responses of both thealogians and witches.[15] At a talk I attended, Ruether argued that 'the goddess wasn't a feminist' and implied that goddess spirituality was not a respectable option for women who care about social justice. Ironically, Ruether was setting out this argument in Ottawa, a city which had recently hosted a meeting of the finance ministers of the G-20 group of nations. Witches,

---

14. The conference was sponsored by the Centre for Women and Christian Traditions at Saint Paul University in Ottawa. Ruether's lectures were 'The Importance of Feminism for Theology Today' and 'An Ecofeminist Theology of Earth Healing'.

15. Raphael, *Introducing Thealogy*.

© The Continuum Publishing Group Ltd 2004.

such as Starhawk, had journeyed from all corners of North America, to make sure that G-20 policies that desecrate the environment and threaten the livelihood of indigenous populations would be brought to the attention of the world. Although copious evidence points to the deep and abiding social concern and compassion in pagan communities, Ruether remains unmoved. Thinking with the metaphors of goddess religion moves many people to fight for the very causes that Ruether herself espouses. What is there about goddess talk and goddess theory that elicits this disparagement?[16]

I suppose that stating 'the goddess was not a feminist' is meant to impugn the egalitarian credentials of those who find the ancient female mythologians inspiring. Christian theology is assumed to be better at fighting poverty and promoting social justice by granting what Ruether sometimes labels 'a preferential option to the poor'. I mistrust this claim since one can effectively argue that the historical record shows Christianity to be responsible for more misery than redemption. As an act of speech, mention of the downtrodden multitudes can function as a muzzle. The claim 'I speak for the poor' is often heard in elite settings where theologians gather. 'The poor' are invoked by certain bourgeois speakers to silence other bourgeois speakers. This is a discursive convention that does 'the poor' no good at all.

Despite her official depreciation of witchy discourse, Ruether appears to mirror some thealogical thought. In the talks I heard she proposed that Christian theology develop an appreciation for the importance of finitude in order to think more effectively about environmental issues. The fact that for years finitude has been a key concept in the published work of witches and thealogians, like Carol Christ, was ignored.[17] Rich resources that could aid Christian reflection about human temporality and limitation are overlooked. Ruether herself has been affected by thealogical discourse, but seems to either repress or forget this influence.

She also declared that the meaning of the Trinity was 'immanental relationality', citing her collaborative work with other Christian theologians to give substance to the claim. Ruether disregarded thealogy, a body of thought and imagery infused with both the immanence and relationality that was being claimed for the Christian Trinity. Ruether had no problem in announcing a new meaning for this ancient symbol of all-

16. For a discussion on ethics in relation to Goddess religion see Carol Christ 'Ethos and Ethics', in *idem, Rebirth of the Goddess* (New York: Routledge, 1998), pp. 160-77.

17. See Carol Christ, *The Laughter of Aphrodite* (San Francisco: HarperSanFrancisco, 1987), pp. 213-27 and *Rebirth of the Goddess*, pp. 113-34. Christ elaborates related themes in her book *She Who Changes* (New York: Palgrave/St Martin, 2003).

male descent and generativity, but she did not take the opportunity to make connections with thealogy.

Ruether told the audience that she recommends sticking with the frameworks of Christianity and other traditional faiths because we already know their pitfalls. If we were to develop new ways of thinking and use new words, we might find ourselves in unknown territory. I suppose this opinion is an indirect acknowledgment of the originality and sense of adventure that is associated with goddess talk. Ruether does not want to explore these discursive spaces. There is no need for her to do so. Her contribution to feminist religious thought is massive even though she stays within the metaphors of Christian God-talk. I have only one request: that she drop that portion of Christian rhetoric that denounces female divinities and their academic and ministerial priestesses.

In her lecture, titled 'An Ecofeminist Theology of Earth Healing', Ruether told her audience that large carnivores, such as lions, are not of primary importance to an ecosystem. It is the little bugs, worms and rodents that are much more essential. Oh no, I thought, now she wants to do away with lions. They better watch out!

Ruether's remark about large carnivores seems to me emblematic of the limits and restrictions that her words would impose. For the last several years, I have spent a few weeks of every summer hiking and camping in places where grizzly bears abound. Watching for signs of these huge animals and catching occasional glimpses of them in the wild is both a terrifying and exhilarating experience. The fact that the bears are able to live in the Canadian Rockies points to the health of that particular portion of the planet. According to Ruether's categories, the grizzlies and other large carnivores are rather superfluous. Her sympathies lean towards the gophers.

I suggest that in Ruether's discursive world, witchy words have teeth and claws. That is why from time to time she voices the opinion that goddess feminism is 'dangerous'.[18] Witchy words can call to mind an oral aggressiveness that suggests a determined hunger and a ravenous desire for survival. Witches' wails can suggest excess, rage, majesty and crazy pride. Why else would creative writers such as Robin Morgan and Xaviére Gauthier call on the metaphor of witchiness to fuel their literary energies?

Imagining feminist theology as a huge discursive ecosystem, might help us to appreciate the value of ideological and linguistic variation. The landscape would be poorer without the carnivores, who, in the

---

18. See Raphael, *Introducing Thealogy*, p. 37 and *passim* for review of Ruether's disparaging comments regarding Goddess religion.

© The Continuum Publishing Group Ltd 2004.

present context, I identify as thealogians, witches, atheists and post-structuralists. Without the lions, and here I will mention that I am a Leo, the carcasses of weak theories and uninspiring metaphors would be left to rot, stifling new growth on the terrain.

The great goddess Cybele chose a pair of lions to pull her chariot. She wanted their muscle and energy to become part of her iconography. Those of us engaged in the enterprise of theory ought to keep the picture of Cybele in mind. Words are our conveyances and we need many potent genres of language to navigate effectively in the wide world. We should not allow our vocabulary to be thoroughly domesticated, de-fanged and de-clawed. To remind ourselves of the value of discursive diversity I suggest we think of ourselves as affiliates of a new feminist group utilizing the honored title of W.I.T.C.H.: Women Insistent on Thealogically Complex Hermeneutics.[19]

---

19. This paper ignited a debate that can be followed in *Feminist Theology* 12.3 (May 2004).

Theaological Reflections on Embodiment

Ruth Mantin

One of the many great contributions that feminist theology has made to the study and practice of religion is the effective challenge it presents to a dominant discourse which places a transcendent, metaphysical God over against the profane realties of a messy, dirty, material world. In dismantling such a dualistic paradigm, feminist theology has affirmed the sacrality of embodiment. Furthermore, feminist theology has, from its outset, been involved with and embedded in wider issues of social justice. It has understood and demonstrated that the construction of religious worldviews is a crucial aspect of the creation, sustenance and perpetuation of oppressive patterns which determine the subjugation and suffering of the majority of the world's population. Analysing, critiquing and re-envisioning 'God-talk' is, therefore, vital to socio/political transformation.

Feminist, womanist and woman-defined theologies, in all their diversity, have made world-opening break-throughs in providing new understandings of what can be meant by spirituality and by the Sacred. They are, however, I believe, constrained by the context in which they operate. They speak from a religious tradition, which carries a heavy weight. It carries centuries of interpretation and inscription that have enshrined a theology of domination. There are, of course, minority and counter-cultural movements within Christian his/herstory that can provide empowering sources and resources. The glorious paradox at the centre of Christianity, which presents a God incarnate in an individual who identified with the marginalized and despised, and was tortured to death as a political subversive, ensures that diversity and critical reconstruction are integral aspects of the Christian tradition. At the same time, however, the voices of possibility provided by these minority sources are almost drowned in the imperious roar of a dominant metanarrative. Christian feminists/womanists inherit a God-talk that was crystallised in the bedrock of classical dualism and metaphysical biophobia. The very fact that Christian feminist theologians are consciously subverting the philosophical assumptions of the dominant theologies is, of itself, valuable. They are, however, in other ways hampered by the need to use the very language, the God-talk, which has framed the worldview that they wish to deconstruct.

Audre Lorde famously identified the difficulty presented by trying to use the master's tools to dismantle the master's house.[1] It was this realisation that led Nelle Morton to abandon 'God' as a dead and redundant symbol and embrace the exorcising and regenerative possibilities of Goddess-talk as metaphoric process.[2] Out of these possibilities has emerged the*a*logy, a term which reflects the affirmation of using female imagery to express the sacred. In this article I wish to argue for a fuller recognition of the contribution that 'Goddess-talk' can make to exploring the sacrality of embodiment in a post-modern world and for further conversation between feminist theologies and thealogies in the undertaking to re-imagine the Sacred and re-articulate expressions of spirituality.

The Potential of Goddess-talk

In the last thirty years, the application of Goddess-talk has emerged as a significant factor in the transformations generated by feminist reconstructions of embodied religion. I wish to maintain, however, that thealogy has a much greater potential to contribute to feminist spiritual discourse than, on the whole, has yet been recognised or fulfilled. Elsewhere, I have attempted to pursue this potential by identifying Goddess-talk as an example of the heteroglossia called for by feminist theorists such as Braidotti[3] and Haraway[4] and by presenting goddesses as feminist figurations that enable epistemological and socio/political transformation.[5] Alongside my exploration of feminist theo/alogical renaming of the sacred, I have examined the implications of this for new understandings of spirituality. Drawing on the work of Carol Christ, I have pursued the possibilities of post-dualistic spiritualities that emerge from attention to women's own narratives. I have become convinced, however, of the need to revisit some of the assumptions of feminist expressions of embodied theo/alogies and spiritualities in the light of post-modern questions

---

1. Audre Lorde, *Sister Outsider: Essays and Speeches* (New York: Crossing Press, 1984), pp. 110-13.
2. Nelle Morton, *The Journey is Home* (Boston: Beacon Press, 1985), pp. 143-45.
3. Rosi Braidotti, *Nomadic Subjects – Embodiment and Sexual Difference in Contemporary Feminist Theory* (New York: Columbia University Press, 1994), p. 8.
4. Donna Haraway, *Simians, Cyborgs, and Women – The Reinvention of Nature* (London: Free Association Books, 1991), pp. 190-233.
5. Ruth Mantin, 'Can Goddesses Travel with Nomads and Cyborgs? Feminist Thealogies in a Postmodern Context', *Feminist Theology* 26 (2001), pp. 21-43.

© The Continuum Publishing Group Ltd 2004.

about the validity of using the category 'woman' and post-structural challenges to the concept of the unified self.

Furthermore, it is now widely recognised within feminist theo/alogy that the category of 'women's experience' has become an increasingly problematic issue precisely because it threatens to thwart the very emancipatory impulses that generated a reclaiming of 'women's experience'. A growing chorus of 'other' women's voices demonstrates that the undifferentiated use of such a term can exclude and negate real women's lived experience. A rigorous consideration of what we mean by female identity and subjectivity is, therefore, central to the socio/political concerns of feminism and not just the esoteric occupation of a privileged academic elite. At the same time, however, there is a real threat that too much concentration on theoretical discourse will remove feminist projects away from actual engagement with the political struggle to improve the lives of oppressed and disadvantaged wo/men. Negotiating routes through these complex and competing demands is the challenge facing feminist theo/alogies in the twenty-first century. I wish to argue that Goddess-talk has something distinctive to offer this process.

I am claiming that Goddess-talk is more open than theology to post-realist notions of immanence, flux and corporeality. This conviction was largely inspired by the reflections of Nelle Morton on the role the metaphoric process generated by the Goddess. For Morton, one of the vital functions of the Goddess as metaphoric image was to shatter the mindset that accepted hierarchical patterns of domination as 'the way things are'. She understood the patriarchal model, realised in the symbol or 'dead metaphor' of a male God, to be responsible for the 'militarised cultures and pervasive hedonistic mentalities' of contemporary political systems.[6]

The role of Goddess as metaphoric image is to 'usher in a new reality'. The iconoclasm of metaphoric movement is followed by 'epiphaneous action'.[7] Morton warned against a Goddess movement that merely brought about the sex change of God without shattering the image of the divine as 'out there', even if she was 'all-loving'. For Morton, to retain such a worldview was failing to exorcise the hold of authoritarianism on one's consciousness'.[8]

Beverley Clack has followed Morton's trajectory to argue that inherent in thealogy is a post-dualistic understanding of spirituality and a non-realist perception of the sacred.[9] She later acknowledged that this

6. Morton, *The Journey is Home*, p. 218.
7. Morton, *The Journey is Home*, p. 218.
8. Morton, *The Journey is Home*, p. 217.
9. Beverley Clack, 'The Denial of Dualism: Thealogical Reflections on the Sexual and the Spiritual', *Feminist Theology* 10 (1995), pp. 102-15.

perception was not an accurate picture of the views of the Goddess movement as a whole.[10] I wish to argue, however, that the possibilities presented by Morton and Clack for the post-metaphysical expressions of Goddess-talk are ones which thealogy needs to pursue. Thealogy can be free of the hold of static dogma and can move with mythogenic agility. This is illustrated in Starhawk's celebrated polyvalence when expressing the meaning of 'Goddess'.

> It all depends on how I feel. When I feel weak, she is someone who can help and protect me. When I feel strong, she is the symbol of my own power. At other times I feel her as the natural energy in my body and the world.[11]

The results of Eller's research into the Goddess movement and my own conversations with Goddess feminists,[12] endorse this approach as characteristic of thealogical reflection. Melissa Raphael has, however, provided compelling arguments for a recognition that many Goddess feminists do retain a realist understanding of the Goddess. For Raphael, this need not rob thealogy of its political potency. On the contrary, she argues that thealogical realism might be necessary for the spiritual feminist project of social transformation. Raphael recognises that thealogy's openness to flux and ambiguity could be classified as the characteristics of a post-modern movement. At the same time, she maintains, these tendencies are held in tension with the liberal, modernist aspirations of feminist intentions to overthrow patriarchy. Raphael views the post-modern features of thealogy as potentially problematic. She fears that they may hinder Goddess feminism's ability to provide effective or persuasive strategies for countering 'the evil of patriarchal disconnection'.[13] Whilst I respect Raphael's analysis and the context out of which she, as a Jewish feminist, speaks, I disagree with her conclusion. I would like to see more evidence of Goddess feminism's post-modern and post-realist potential expressed in its refiguration of the Sacred. I would argue that it

---

10. Beverley Clack, 'The Many-Named Queen of All: Thealogy and the Concept of the Goddess', in Deborah Sawyer and Diane Collier (eds.), *Is There a Future for Feminist Theology?* (Sheffield: Sheffield Academic Press, 1999), pp. 150-59.

11. Personal communication between Starhawk and Carol Christ quoted in 'Why Women Need the Goddess: Phenomenological Psychological and Political Reflections', in Carol P. Christ and Judith Plaskow (eds.), *Womanspirit Rising: A Reader in Feminist Religion* (San Francisco: Harper & Row, 1979), pp. 278-79.

12. Ruth Mantin, *Thealogies in Process: the Role of Goddess-talk in Contemporary Feminist Spirituality* (Unpublished PhD dissertation).

13. Melissa Raphael, 'Truth in Flux: Goddess Feminism as a Late Modern Religion', *Religion* 26 (1996), pp. 199-221.

is precisely in its anti-foundational manifestation that thealogy can disrupt the boundaries that are set to separate and suppress.

Refiguring the Sacred

Making such claims for thealogy is not to deny that feminist theologies have made vital contributions to a refiguration of the divine which moves it from the impassive, immutable distance of classical theology into the joy and suffering of the material world. Ruether, when she produced her groundbreaking analysis of the relationship between sexism and God-talk,[14] recognised the breadth of the range of socio/political implications ensuing from the metaphysical paradigm of classical theology. Ruether demonstrated how the 'hierarchy of being' on which this paradigm was constructed provided the model for domination and subjugation for all other hierarchies. For Ruether, therefore, the process of removing the Sacred from its position 'beyond' the physical and into primal matter is central to the social and economic transformation she desires. A consequence of this move is the need to relinquish a concept of immortality. Ruether has since said that, when discussing her theories in talks and lectures, the aspect that provokes the most reaction and hostility from her listeners is the suggestion that they are 'deprived' of their right to eternal life after death.[15] I share Ruether's analysis that the social transformation envisaged by a renaming of the sacred requires a willingness to relinquish attachment to a metaphysical worldview.

Not all feminist theologians go as far as Ruether in framing a materialist theology, but most share her passion to provide a wider re-visioning of notions of the Sacred. Mary Grey has recently provided an overview of the implications of feminist re-imaging of God.[16] Her survey, consciously informed by her own perspective, presents images of God which move beyond the dualistic assumptions of classical theology. This is an embodied God, immanent in the material world, in the physical struggles of oppressed communities and in the individual's passion for justice. This God defies the restrictions of classical transcendence and is present *in* the suffering, the disadvantaged and subjugated. In order to counter images of a distant, impassive divinity, Grey is prepared to envision a God who responds to the ambiguity and tragedy of unexplained

---

14. Rosemary Radford Ruether, *Sexism and God-talk: Toward A Feminist Theology* (Boston: Beacon Press, 1983).

15. This comment was made by Ruether during a conversation at the American Academy of Religion conference, Nashville, Tennessee, November 2000.

16. Mary Grey, *Introducing Feminist Images of God* (Sheffield: Sheffield Academic Press, 2001).

suffering. For Grey, the image of Sophia facilitates the revisioning of God generated by feminist challenges to dualistic patterns of oppression. Grey's overview of the passionate creativity involved in feminist theologies' imaging of God illustrates the challenges facing those who operate within the framework of God-talk.[17] They recognise that one of most debilitating images with which they struggle is the transcendent God of classical theology. Thealogy has responded to this by an overwhelming emphasis on the Sacred as immanent. Within theology, however, feminists are obliged to retain some understanding of divine transcendence. This has its advantages in that, as a result, feminist theologies have produced very creative and enabling interpretations of this concept. Carter Heyward has brought the notion down from the metaphysical distance and into relationality by arguing that the 'trans' of transcendence can refer to the movement 'across' and 'between' rather than 'out of'.[18] When constructing an urban ecofeminism that resonated with the political struggles of the wo/men of Latin America and with the Catholic Christianity within which they are situated, Ivone Gebara presents a reconsideration of traditional understandings of transcendence. It becomes an affirmation that experience of the divine cannot be confined within the words we use to express it. In this sense, transcendence becomes a quality which is not just 'out there' but within every human's reality.[19]

These examples demonstrate that feminist theology is refiguring traditional notions of divine transcendence. A significant aspect of this process is to question the very assumption of posing a binary opposition between immanence and transcendence. In challenging the dualism of immanence and transcendence, Jantzen offers a 'pantheist symbolic' as one which promotes 'a feminist recognition of the divine as a horizon of becoming, exploring the embodied, earthed, female divine as "the perfection of our subjectivity"'.[20]

The rejection of such a dualism is even more apparent in thealogy[21] and I do not deny its value. I respect feminist theological strategies to

---

17. In her survey, Grey acknowledges the valuable contribution offered by thealogy to refigurations of embodied divinity. She does, however, voice reservations about the Goddess movement's ability, or motivation to address issues of globalised social injustice.

18. Carter Heyward, *Our Passion for Justice – Images of Power, Sexuality and Liberation* (Cleveland, OH: The Pilgrim Press, 1984).

19. Ivone Gebara, *Longing for Running Water* (Philadelphia: Fortress Press, 1999), pp. 153, 167.

20. Grace M. Jantzen, *Becoming Divine: Towards a Feminist Philosophy of Religion* (Manchester: Manchester University Press, 1998), p. 275.

21. See e.g., Starhawk, *The Spiral Dance: A Rebirth of the Ancient Religion of The Great Goddess* (San Francisco: Harper & Row, 1978); Merlin Stone, *When God Was A Woman*

appropriate the concept on their own terms and appreciate the possible dangers of re-inscribing the essentialist connection between 'woman' and 'immanence'.²² On the other hand, I still question, in view of its far-reaching devastation, how helpful it is to retain the image of divine transcendence.

Another, related, dichotomy which is challenged by feminist theo/alogy is one which posits 'realism' over against 'non-realism'. Jantzen and Clack address the possibility of overcoming such a position in the light of a feminist refiguring of the sacred. Jantzen finds the realist/anti-realist debate unhelpful and maintains the value of recognising that:

> there is every reason to suspend questions of truth in the interests of allowing more scope to the creative imagination, and seeing to what extent a feminist projection of a female divine might help shift the ground of what has too often been a highly oppressive concept of God. This is not least because such a shifting of ground will involve a re-visioning of truth itself and how it should be pursued.²³

The emphasis in thealogy on Goddess as symbol and as self, lends it to non-realist expressions of the sacred. As discussed above, Melissa Raphael and Beverley Clack have debated the extent to which non-realism is vital to the imaginal shift envisioned by thealogy.²⁴ In the light of this debate, Clack suggests:

(New York: Dial Press, 1976). Published in Britain as *The Paradise Papers* (London: Virago, 1976); Cynthia Eller, *Living in the Lap of the Goddess: The Feminist Spirituality Movement in America* (New York: Crossroad, 1993); Asphodel Long, 'The One or the Many: The Great Goddess Revisited', *Feminist Theology* 15 (1997), pp. 13-29; Carol Christ, *Rebirth of the Goddess – Finding Meaning in Feminist Spirituality* (New York: Addison Wesley, 1997).

22. Simone de Beauvoir, *The Second Sex* (Harmondsworth: Penguin Books, 1972 [1948]) defined the feminist project as the need for women to escape their association with immanence. Whilst respecting her position as a pioneer of feminism, feminist theorists are now questioning her attitudes to immanence and transcendence and the notions of subjectivity on which they are based e.g. Judith Butler, *Gender Trouble: Feminism and the Subversion of Identity* (London: Routledge); Elizabeth Spelman, *Inessential Woman* (Boston: Beacon Press, 1990); Braidotti, *Nomadic Subjects*. Several feminist theo/alogians have responded to and re-interpreted de Beauvoir's claims, e.g., Mary Daly, *Beyond God the Father – Toward a Philosophy of Women's Liberation* (Boston: Beacon Press, 1973); Catherine Keller, *From a Broken Web – Separation Sexism and Self* (Boston; Beacon Press, 1986). More recently, Jantzen has addressed this issue in relation to Irigaray's concept of a 'sensible transcendence…a transcendence which is wholly immanent, not in opposition to the flesh but as the projected horizon for our (embodied) becoming'. See Jantzen, *Becoming Divine*, p. 271.

23. Jantzen, *Becoming Divine*, p. 192.

24. Clack, 'The Many-Named Queen of All'; Melissa Raphael, *Monotheism in*

Thealogy challenges the very way in which we consider the universe and our place in it, and that challenge may also have the effect of breaking down the barriers between people who might have thought themselves as realist or non-realist. Perhaps the Goddess is telling us that such distinctions do not do justice to the complex ways in which religious language works.[25]

In a move similar to that of Clack, I wish to question the validity of a realist/non-realist split within a thealogical paradigm whilst maintaining the worth of challenging metaphysical dualisms. I therefore prefer to signify my position as 'post-realist'.[26]

Feminist theo/alogies have shifted the world out of a dualistic paradigm. They have envisioned images of the divine that are embodied and present in the flux and fluidity of lived experience. I welcome further movement in that shift, beyond realist and metaphysical definitions, allowing a notion of the sacred which leaves behind a reliance on self-referential stability. This movement has been anticipated in the concept of 'enacting the divine', recognised by Grigg as a sympathetic and enthusiastic observer.[27] I wish to carry this metaphor further. In following Morton's trajectory, I recognise the need to discard images of metaphysical reality. When the metaphysical trappings of immutability have been removed, we are left with an expression of the sacred as process. A vital aspect of this process, however, is that it is *relational*. This was suggested by Daly's configuration of Goddess as Verb.[28] Notably, the verb is an intransitive one. It therefore has no object, it does not attempt to define the other. It does have a subject. That subject, however, is not fixed. It is constantly in relation to the verb. This movement in relation conveys something of what I understand the sacred to be—a process which releases movement, defies boundaries and enables relationality. To recognise the enactive and relational aspect of the sacred opens possibilities for understanding sacrality as performative.

Contemporary Feminist Goddess Religion: A Betrayal of Early Thealogical Non-Realism?', in D. Sawyer and D. Collier (eds.), *Is There a Future for Feminist Theology?*, pp. 139-49.

25. Clack, 'The Many-Named Queen of All', pp. 153-54.

26. My use of this term resulted from a conversation with Carol Christ in March 2001. Christ challenged my view that my position was 'non-realist' and in opposition to hers when I still spoke in terms of relation and communication with forms of life such as the sea. I found her argument compelling and considered that the prefix 'post' better conveyed both a distinction from, and a continuum with, her own view of Goddess as 'personal presence'.

27. Richard Grigg, *When God Becomes Goddess: The Transformation of American Religion* (New York: Continuum, 1995).

28. Mary Daly, *Gyn/Ecology: The Metaethics of Radical Feminism* (Boston: Beacon Press, 1978).

Although I am calling for an understanding of divinity as performative, I still, like Daly, argue for the relevance of Goddess-talk in expressing this process. Because I am claiming that relationality is inherent in a figuration of the sacred as process, I maintain that metaphors of personal language are appropriate to use when constructing an imaginary around it.[29] In particular, female imagery can help to exorcise from narratives of the sacred the imperialist, colonising associations of metaphysical, realist expressions of deity. Feminist thealogies can generate such imagery in the construction of a religious symbolic. This was apparent in the responses of the women with whom I inter/viewed.[30] They affirmed the ways in which Goddess myths functioned to counter the debilitating effects of patriarchy and to generate alternative patterns of relation and socio/political structure. The responses also conveyed an understanding that these myths were not fixed but could travel with them on their own journeys. Goddess-talk infuses the narratives of the sacred with an openness to plurality and ambiguity. The imagery and mythologies of Goddesses can contribute further to this process by re-membering the connections between the demonisation of female authority and the construction of 'monsters'. A thealogy which affirms the sacrality of monsters might have something to offer attempts to challenge the attitudes which dis-able the different.[31] When developing their body theo/alogy, Lisa Isherwood and Elisabeth Stuart consider the important challenges presented to notions of embodiment by the experience of people with disabilities.[32] They relate this to the dangers they perceive in thealogy of

---

29. This is not to deny the value of *im*personal symbolism in figuring the divine. My emphasis on immanence echoes thealogical and ecofeminist calls for the resacralisation of the earth and the possibility of any object or element conveying the presence of the sacred. I wish here to justify the validity of Goddess-talk in expressing the sacred as process, not to endorse anthropocentrism.

30. Steinar Kvale coins the term 'inter/view' in his book *InterViews: An Introduction to Qualitative Research Interviewing* (Thousand Oaks, CA: Sage, 1996). Here he emphasises the constructive nature of the knowledge(s) created through the interaction of partners in the interview conversation. I adopted this methodology when inter/viewing with women's narratives as part of my PhD dissertation (*Thealogies in Process: the Role of Goddess-talk in Contemporary Feminist Spirituality*).

31. Jackie Leach Scully, 'When Embodiment Isn't Good', *Theology and Sexuality* 8 (1998), quoted in L. Isherwood and E. Stuart (eds.), *Introducing Body Theology* (Sheffield: Sheffield Academic Press, 1998), p. 94.

32. Isherwood and Stuart note that, for people with disabilities, the power of renaming is a vital factor in the struggle for social justice and against social stereotyping. There are therefore a range of terms presented by the differently abled to describe themselves over against the dominant discourse which renders them less capable and less human than the 'norm'. Isherwood and Stuart explain that they use the phrase

presenting a romanticised and 'pure' understanding of embodiment, linked to a distrust of technology. Drawing on Haraway's dichotomy of goddess and cyborg, they argue that a cyborg figuration provides more potential for people with disabilities for whom the blurred boundary between human body and technology is often a lived reality. They also refer to Nancy Eiesland's liberatory theology of disability. Out of an analysis of the lived experience of people with disabilities, Eiesland explores new possibilities for expressing the central Christian concept of incarnation. She presents her epiphany of a disabled God, revealed by the survivor Christ whose 'impaired' body is the incarnation of the full contingency of human life.[33] I would want to argue that Goddess-talk which questions notions of 'wholeness' and which affirms the sacred in the ambiguities of embodiment and in the monstrous other might also contribute to a thealogy of disability.[34]

I share the doubts of Isherwood and Stuart that neither thealogy nor Christian theology has yet developed the necessary processes to attempt the crucial task of responding to the life and death challenges posed by attitudes to physical and mental disabilities. Such challenges, they suggest require us to 'face up to the terror of otherness'.[35] What thealogy can, perhaps, do is to de-monstrate the extent to which the performative sacred refigures the boundaries between the Absolute and the Other. In so doing, Goddess-talk sacralises those deemed monstrous by the purveyors of dominant discourse. This transgressive sacrality also exposes the oppressive structures that determine the confines within which the 'others' exist. It enables the alliances and strategies that can work in solidarity with the political struggles of communities crushed by globalised injustice.

It is clear from the above that many feminist theologians and thealogians are renegotiating the boundaries between concepts of immanence

---

'people with disabilities' because this is the term used by Nancy Eiesland in her groundbreaking book *The Disabled God: Toward a Liberatory Theology of Disability* (Nashville: Abingdon Press, 1994).

33. Eiesland, *The Disabled God*, pp. 99-100, quoted in Isherwood and Stuart, *Introducing Body Theology*, pp. 91-93.

34. I appreciate that there is a danger in using Goddess narratives such as those of Lilith and Medusa to affirm the sacrality of monsters and the demonised other if the monstrous nature of these Goddesses is perceived as the distortion of patriarchy, disguising their 'true' beauty. I would, nevertheless, maintain that the association between monsters and Goddesses presents the potential for challenging narratives which dis-able the different and for seeking effective responses to the terror of otherness.

35. Isherwood and Stuart, *Introducing Body Theology*, p. 94.

© The Continuum Publishing Group Ltd 2004.

and transcendence. These negotiations are undertaken not to indulge in esoteric mind-games but to sacralise the world in a political act of disruption and restoration. I would, however, maintain that feminist theologians are sometimes hampered in the pursuit of their arguments by the realist, metaphysical trappings of the 'God' language they use. The familial ties that bind God-talk to metaphysics, dualism and the philosophical assumptions of modernity are very strong. Goddesses have far more freedom to wander outside the family circle. They can more easily facilitate a nomadic consciousness. Their connections with shape-shifters make it much more difficult to fix them within a system. Their relationships with monsters allow them to include rather than marginalise the other. I appreciate that I am tending to group together realism, transcendence and metaphysics in a coalescent lump. At the same time I would justify categorising these three concepts into an alliance, I do perceive an inevitable connection between them. Following Braidotti, I would argue that metaphysics is a 'political ontology'[36] which, whilst devaluing the material, also conceals the cultural construction of discourses of the divine and locates a distant, literalised deity beyond the transience and ambiguity of lived experience.

To determine the location of the sacred is a political act. I am, therefore, convinced of the need for feminist theo/alogies to travel further in recognising the socio/political implications of constructing our own post-metaphysical narratives of the sacred and in enacting performative sacrality.

Subjectivity, Identity and Expressions of Embodied Spiritualities

Alongside such a project, I place the need for further explorations of the implications of post-Cartesian interrogations of the notion of identity and understandings of subjectivity as process for enabling new expressions of embodied spiritualities. When I first encountered the work of Rosi Braidotti, I found it difficult to appreciate her argument that the 'gesture that binds a fractured self to the performative illusion of unity', was an act of violent force.[37] I have since been convinced by feminist arguments that Descartes' narrative of the unified, separate self was constructed upon a correlation between the 'self' and the situation of elite maleness. Furthermore, this model determined the Enlightenment projects of emancipation, positing the male, elite subject as the norm, against which notions of equality were measured. The 'unity' of the self

---

36. See e.g., Braidotti, *Nomadic Subjects*, p. 108.
37. Braidotti, *Nomadic Subjects*, p. 12.

was inscribed by positing a unified 'essential' self, commensurate with androcentric and colonial presuppositions, which was capable of affixing 'attributes' such as 'gender' or 'race'. This construct of the self was linked to the project of Western rationalism, which was perceived as a relentless march of progress towards an ideal 'wholeness' which lay beyond the fragmentation of imperfect and perspectival perceptions. A recognition of the damaging effects of such models has provoked a move within feminism away from a notion of 'equality', which presupposes an absolute with which to equate, and the consideration of appropriate strategies with which to respond to 'difference'. It has also prompted many feminists to argue the socio/political implications of challenging the fictive unity of the self.

One feminist thinker who has perhaps had the most impact on the exploration of this challenge is Judith Butler. Her groundbreaking book, *Gender Trouble*,[38] confronts and disputes one of the founding themes of feminism, the notion of 'woman'. She sets herself the question

> What new shape of politics emerges when identity as a common ground no longer constrains the discourse on feminist politics? ...to what extent does the effort to locate a common identity as the foundation for a feminist politics preclude a radical enquiry into the political construction and regulation of identity itself?[39]

For Butler, to hold on to the category 'woman' is to collude with other oppressive narratives. She maintains that there is a 'connection between political assumptions that there must be a universal basis for feminism and efforts to colonise and appropriate non-Western cultures' this allows an explanation of gender oppression 'as symptomatic of an essential, non-Western barbarism'.[40] She argues that this model of subjectivity also supports colonial assumptions by complying with a construct of the subject that operates through 'the exclusion of those who fail to conform to unspoken normative requirements of the subject'.[41] Butler's focus, however, is upon the social construction of identity in relation to gender and sexuality. Butler disputes the widely accepted distinction between 'gender' and 'sex' and maintains that 'gender is not to culture as sex is to nature'.[42] Butler argues that all humans have the potential to be polysexual and that sexual identity and 'gender' are both socially constructed. She suggests that the category of woman as a coherent and stable subject

---

38. Judith Butler, *Gender Trouble* (London: Routledge, 1990).
39. Butler, *Gender Trouble*, p. ix.
40. Butler, *Gender Trouble*, p. 3.
41. Butler, *Gender Trouble*, p. 5.
42. Butler, *Gender Trouble*, p. 6.

is itself an 'unwitting regulation and reification of gender relations'. Such regulation, she argues, can only operate within 'the context of the heterosexual matrix'.[43] Butler contrasts the humanist conception of the subject as a substantive person who is the bearer of various essential and non-essential 'attributes' (of which, gender would be one) with a social theory of gender. Here, gender would be understood as a *relation* among socially constituted subjects in an historically specific set of relations. She develops this argument further, however, to maintain that gender is 'an identity tenuously constituted in time, instituted in an exterior space through a *stylized repetition of acts*'.[44] Butler concludes, therefore, that 'gender', as a constructed identity, is enacted as 'a performative accomplishment'.[45] Butler's theory of identity, and gender as a feature of that identity, as 'performative', presents challenging but stimulating possibilities for feminist theo/alogies.[46]

The legacy of Western philosophy is the desire to identify the 'self' with fixed categories that are separate and self-authenticating. In order to be faithful to their desire to subvert the patterns of domination that oppress women in all their diverse contexts, feminists need to re-examine their 'dreams of a common language' between all women. This entails a willingness to face the challenges of rethinking subjectivity in order to relinquish the residues of Western rationality's dreams of unity.

I would argue that thealogy's openness to plurality and process equips it to assist in narrating such challenges. Despite her reservations about the post-modern tendencies of thealogy, Raphael quotes Naomi Goldenberg with approval when she relates the notion of a single, fixed religious identity to patterns of violence and oppression based on the centrality of tribal loyalties. Raphael claims that 'for Goldenberg, and other spiritual feminists, feminism is about the need to feel the empathy, involvement and identity beyond our particular tribe that is vital to the renunciation of control and dominance and to the cause of global peace. Tribalism is threatened by those who enjoy multiple, connected identities, by the female sense of diversity within self-hood'.[47] Goldenberg therefore argues that:

---

43. Butler, *Gender Trouble*, p. 6.
44. Butler, *Gender Trouble*, p. 140.
45. Butler, *Gender Trouble*, p. 141.
46. Butler's ideas are being most explicitly appropriated by feminist theologies which relate to Queer theory, e.g., Elizabeth Stuart, *Religion is a Queer Thing* (Sheffield: Sheffield Academic Press, 1997); Marcella Althaus-Reid, *Indecent Theology: Theological Perversions in Sex, Gender and Politics* (London: Routledge, 2001).
47. Melissa Raphael, *Introducing Thealogy: Discourse on the Goddess* (Sheffield: Sheffield Academic Press, 1999a), p. 27.

the world needs more people who can feel several loyalties, several affinities, *several identities.*⁴⁸

Raphael argues that Goddess feminists can respond to such a need and I agree. When I argue for a dismantling of the Cartesian unified self, I do, however, appreciate that this is not without its problems. I have sympathy with those who claim that fragmentation has been all too apparent a feature of women's experiences within patriarchy and that to reinscribe disintegration is disastrous. I take these claims very seriously although it is not possible to acknowledge fully here the scope of the debate. Similarly, I recognise that feminist claims to 'wholeness' are by no means synonymous with the dreams of unity voiced by Western rationalism.

Lucy Tatman, for instance, provides some moving and insightful reflections on wholeness and at-one-ment in relation to the practice of self-mutilation.⁴⁹ Her encounter with women who experience this provoked her to re-examine her denial of a body/mind separation. She argued that sometimes women need to disassociate their 'self' from the body that had suffered abuse. Tatman suggested that when they produced pain in their own bodies, it was an expression that these women needed to demonstrate to themselves that they were able to 'feel something rather than nothing'. Tatman termed as 'whole enough' the state that these women need to experience. She maintains that a theological concept of atonement must speak to this human yearning for wholeness. At the same time, she is anxious to distance this notion of wholeness from a 'longing for a merged unity with a transcendent deity' and from a notion of the individual centred on a construct of the self as wholly separate and autonomous. Indeed, Tatman relates her concept of 'whole-enough' to change and process.

> Wholeness has to do with individual human integrity, the integration within oneself of all of one's life experiences, even (perhaps particularly) her most painful. A yearning for wholeness is an on-going longing; it's about reaching into one's past, feeling that past into the present, transforming that past in different ways at different times, and then taking the past and present into the future with oneself. *At no time is the process fully completed*; we muddle along as best we can, striving to be and become more or less whole-enough to keep muddling sometimes giving, sometimes being given a helpful nudge along the way.⁵⁰

48. N. Goldenberg, *Resurrecting the Body: Feminism, Religion and Psychoanalysis* (New York: Crossroad, 1990), pp. 64-67, cited in Raphael 1999, p. 27 (italics mine).
49. Lucy Tatman, 'The Yearning to be Whole-enough or to Feel Something Not Nothing: A Feminist Theological Consideration of Self-mutilation as an Act of Atonement', *Feminist Theology* 17 (1998), pp. 25-38.
50. Tatman, 'The Yearning to be Whole-enough', p. 35.

I appreciate Tatman's attempt, one she acknowledges as difficult, to express a notion of 'wholeness as process'. I also acknowledge that 'hopes for wholeness', expressed by spiritual feminists such as Kathleen Zappone, do not equate such wholeness with perfection nor with linear aspirations. Instead, she refers to a 'tidal movement of ebb and flow'. Like other relational theo/alogians, for Zappone the key to feminist spirituality is an awareness of relatedness and mutuality.[51] Furthermore, I am aware that thealogy presents the possibility of rethinking 'wholeness' further with its narratives of Goddess as 'The One *and* the Many'.[52] It also provides images of the Virgin aspects of Goddess that express a sense of 'being whole to oneself' in contrast to the need for female identities to be defined by male constructs. This is in stark contrast to the construction of Christian doctrines about the virginity of Mary, built around the necessity to distance her from any aroma of female sexuality and to ensure her unbroken hymen. Instead, thealogy offers narratives of goddesses such as Athene/Diana who were free to express their sexuality in multiple ways whist maintaining the integrity of their virginity. Whilst I recognise the potential of all such images for rethinking wholeness, and appreciate the debilitating effects of fragmentation, I would still want to reconsider images that suggest unity with regard to the nature of subjectivity and, thereby, of spirituality because of their tendency, discussed above, to exclude and negate.

Subjectivity as process, I would nevertheless argue, does not have to convey the disintegration of a fractured self. It recognises the fluidity and multiplicity of subjectivity but retains a sense of continuum. Central to feminist expressions of spirituality is recognition of connectedness and relation. As Keller[53] and Braidotti[54] suggest, identity can be mapped from this process, but only retrospectively, the process is ongoing. If we accept the damage caused by humanist concepts of a substantive, essential 'self' to which additional 'attributes' can be attached, there is no 'core' to which one can return in order to affirm identity and no ultimate destination to which the process must travel. This need not mean, however, that identity cannot exist. The devastating effects of alienation and disintegration are experienced when there is no sense of relation with the process of one's own subjectivity and/or no sense of connection with

---

51. Kathleen Zappone, *The Hope for Wholeness* (London: Twenty Third Publications, 1991).

52. E.g., Asphodel Long, 'The One or the Many, The Great Mother Revisited', *Feminist Theology* 15 (1997), pp. 13-29.

53. Catherine Keller, *From a Broken Web: Separation, Sexism and the Self* (Boston: Beacon Press, 1986), p. 194.

54. Braidotti, *Nomadic Subjects*.

the relational subjectivity of others. I would therefore underline the importance of the 'trans' in transformation to indicate relation 'across' subjectivities. I would also suggest that 're-membering' our subjectivity as process involves the very opposite of disintegration.

Feminist approaches to the study and practice of religion have made vital contributions to understandings of the connection between narrative, identity and spirituality, as well as between spirituality, sexuality and politics. In her groundbreaking work on women's narratives as spiritual quest, Carol Christ provided an interpretive model for exploring feminist spirituality — Nothingness — Awakening — Insight — New Naming.[55] The way in which Christ then expressed such a quest — as moving 'towards wholeness' — could now be open to criticism for its linear and teleological assumptions. If, however, it is refigured as an ongoing, spiralling movement which expects no destination in unity,[56] it can still articulate a spirituality which is challenging the boundaries of identity and of difference. I would argue that post-structural expressions of subjectivity as multiple and fluctuating present real possibilities for re-visioning embodied, post-dualistic spiritualities. I would argue for the value of exploring further the potential of images that express as spirituality the many changes and relations which constitute that which we trans-form and re-member as subjectivity and identity. To raise such possibilities is to recognise that they demand further interrogation in relation to meaningful and enabling expressions of the sacred. Not least, they require further exploration into their relationship with women-defined theo/alogies of the Majority World, with searching questions about the currency of concepts such as 'evil' and 'justice' and with political strategies to address the human and ecological devastation wreaked by capitalist globalisation. I desire the opportunity to participate in conversations with wo/men who struggle with such concerns.

---

55. Carol Christ, *Diving Deep and Surfacing: Women Writers on Spiritual Quest* (Boston: Beacon Press, 1980), pp. 119-31.

56. Christ recognised this and expressed her *Odyssey with the Goddess* as a 'serpentine path' which 'does not ever come to a point'. She speaks of 'not the goal, but the journey'. See Carol Christ, *Odyssey with the Goddess: A Spiritual Quest in Crete* (New York: Continuum, 1995), p. 163.

© The Continuum Publishing Group Ltd 2004.

Exploding Mystery: Feminist Theology and the Sacramental

Elizabeth Stuart

The inauguration of the first chair in feminist liberation theology in the UK is certainly a time to rejoice in the glorious gain of feminist theology but it may also be an opportune time to ask whether anything may have been lost in the process of that gain. I believe that European and North American Christian feminist theology has largely conceded the mystery, the invisible, the sacramental to patriarchy when there was absolutely no need for it do so and indeed good theological and political reasons exist to resist such a concession. In many respects, feminist theology may be understood as a form of liberal Protestantism, the Enlightenment's daughter. Post-modern critical theory demands that feminist theology re-examine some of its central 'orthodoxies', and I wish to contend, enables feminist theology to reclaim the mysterious and the sacramental from the stranglehold of patriarchy and thereby rescue itself from the weaknesses of liberal Protestantism.

Deadly Demythologisation

Certain 'orthodoxies' have become quickly established in European and North American feminist theologies. Ideas that have come to be accepted as truth, go largely unexamined and uncontested and become a defining characteristic of feminist theology. One of these orthodoxies is that classical Christianity has constructed humanity and divinity as a dualism that, like all dualisms, has produced wrong relation and must be overcome.[1] Alternative theologies are constructed in which the divine is rendered radically horizontal, immanent in all things, sacralising all life. The existence of a divine reality behind and beyond the one in which we live and move is therefore denied along with notions of a life after death and the possibilities of miracles. Christology is re-centred away from Jesus and he is reduced to an exemplar of a christic way of being, a living out of 'erotic power', that is, right relational power which is identified

---

1. See, e.g., Carter Heyward, *Speaking of Christ: A Lesbian Feminist Voice* (Cleveland, OH: The Pilgrim Press, 1989), pp. 18-22.

with the divine.[2] Feminist theology therefore tends to engage in a radical form of demythologisation. Bultmann thought that it was impossible to believe in the demons and the spirits of the New Testament whilst switching on the electric light and listening to the wireless; feminist theologians maintain that it is impossible to fight against patriarchy and its dualistic construction of the universe and hold on to a sense of the radical otherness of the divine. There are, however, problems inherent in such a stance. A refusal to recognise a duality (which is not the same as a dualism) between divinity and humanity collapses the divine into human experience to the point that it disappears or virtually disappears. Complete disappearance leaves us alone and self-sufficient:

> no one can help us avoid our own pain. No one else can stop the suffering of broken heartedness in our world but our own courage and willingness to act in the midst of the awareness of our own fragility. No one else can die for us or bring justice, liberation and healing.[3]

So we become dependent solely upon ourselves and upon the divine that is somehow experienced in our struggle to generate power for life. We are left to pull ourselves up by our own bootstraps. Such a vision reflects the middle-class western self that has the means of taking care of themselves and of others, it is a self which has confidence in its own ability to organise and change the world. This is the very same self that lay behind liberal Protestantism albeit with slight modifications, in particular an emphasis upon relationality and connectedness. It is a self that absorbs all into itself including the divine and others under the guise of relationality. The virtual disappearance of the divine allows it to be called forth at will as a dimension of the middle-class self to underpin it but never to challenge it, because the divine is allowed no life of its own. Theology ceases to be theology and becomes instead a purely hermeneutical enterprise, largely deconstructive in character or shrunk to ethical reflection. These orthodoxies and their practical outcomes are no help to the non-western middle-class self, to those who do have the resources to absorb the world into their own selves or to that western middle-class self when it itself is faced with something it cannot absorb, death being the most obvious example of an experience which cannot be colonised. The danger of feminist theology is that instead of sacralising all reality it actually ends up deadening reality by thickening the material order so that no other reality can survive within it. This is not a mistake made by our sister thealogians.

2. See, e.g., Rita Nakashima Brock, *Journeys By Heart: A Christology of Erotic Power* (New York: Crossroad, 1991).
3. Brock, *Journeys By Heart*, p. 106.

The Magic of the Goddess

In contrast to most feminist theologians, many thealogians have not only retained a mystical dimension to their discourse and practice but also argued that it is essential to the work of resistance against patriarchy. For the thealogian the universe pulsates with unseen forces, 'the sacred is a beneficent creative power that can be ritually "tapped into" for healing and empowerment against evil'.[4] The tapping into takes place through magic, an art in which sacred energy is gathered and focused by the will. The women's peace camp at Greenham Common could be understood to have been the most prominent recent manifestation of women's magical arts. There ritual actions such as encircling the air force base or attaching rags soaked in menstrual blood to the perimeter fence were designed to challenge and change the energies of violence, destruction and patriarchy and, of course, it is possible to claim that it worked. The weapons of destruction have been removed from Greenham and the women have departed, their sacred work having been completed. A belief in magic, in mysterious unseen forces, that can be summoned up and directed empowers; it allows for the possibility that apparently small gestures or ritual actions can, in fact, change the world. It accepts the mysterious otherness of the divine, the grace of disconnection between the human and the divine, while allowing for the possibility that humanity can cooperate with the mysterious forces in the work of redeeming or recreating the world.

The Re-enchantment of the World

Melissa Raphael has noted that the thealogical concern with magic may be understood as part of the post-modern project to re-enchant the world:

> Whereas positivist modernity confined the 'real' to the observable properties of matter, post modernity has reunited energy, imagination and matter. The world is (re)opened to magical suggestion. The energies of heavenly and human bodies, flesh and the cosmos, are (re)made continuous with one another.[5]

Zygmunt Bauman identified three elements to the post-modern re-sacralising of the world.[6] The first is the dethroning of reason that creates

---

4. Melissa Raphael, *Thealogy and Embodiment: The Post-Patriarchal Reconstruction of Female Sacrality* (Sheffield: Sheffield Academic Press, 1996), p. 48.
5. Raphael, *Thealogy and Embodiment*, p. 27.
6. Zygmunt Bauman, *Postmodern Ethics* (Princeton, NJ: Princeton University Press, 1993).

the space for the revalorisation of the non-rational, the emotional and the embodied and the re-emergence of the transcendent. The second element is the re-emergence of the Other as the radically different and beyond possession. This creates space for the mysterious, the unexplainable and the unnameable. It acknowledges the possibility of a duality without dualism and a disconnection without alienation. And finally, the universal and objective is replaced by a much more particular and relative approach to ethics. Graham Ward notes that this re-enchantment is accompanied by a new model of selfhood, 'The self is now part of a much larger economy of desire. It is not simply self-defining, it is also defined'.[7] This re-enchantment of the world is evident in first world popular culture in pre-occupation with angels, aliens and other worlds. In one of the most theologically analysed films of the twentieth century, *The Matrix* (1999) the central character, Neo, is presented with two pills. The blue pill will end the story for him and he will return to the 'reality' he knows and functions in unaware of any other dimensions to existence. The red pill, however, will render him forever conscious of the matrix, of the unreality of 'reality', of different layers of existence. Postmodernism presents us with the metaphorical red pill, opening up to our culture again the Otherness of the divine, the space of transcendence, the magic realm of the mysterious. Feminist theology has not tended to take up the invitation to step into this aporia having conceded the other world to patriarchy long ago. My contention is that feminist theology has nothing to lose and everything to gain from stepping out of deadly grip of liberal Protestantism into a space of Otherness and mystery.

Stepping into Incense

Some feminist theology makes the mistake of representing the Christian tradition as constructing a Christology that assumes the eternal uniqueness and Otherness of Christ.[8] The Christian tradition is more complex and subtle than this in its sacramental system it manages to hold together two things: the Otherness of the divine and the incorporation of humanity into that divine life. Feminist theology has made the classic mistake of liberal Protestantism in 'doing' Christology from the foundation of contemporary notions of what it means to be human so that Christ is reduced to an idealised image of ourselves and our aspirations. The

---

7. Graham Ward, *Theology and Contemporary Critical Theory* (Basingstoke: Macmillan; New York: St Martin's Press, 2nd edn, 2000), p. 119.
8. See, e.g., Lisa Isherwood, *Liberating Christ: Exploring the Christologies of Contemporary Liberation Movements* (Cleveland, OH: The Pilgrim Press, 1999).

tradition however, demands a different approach, that we look to Christ as our model of what it means to be truly human. To be taken up into the divine life through the sacramental system, is also to be taken into authentic humanity, there is no dualism between the two although the Otherness of the divine is preserved by the mystery conveyed through the ritual preventing an easy and dangerous identification between the divine and the human.

Feminist theo-praxis has conceded to neo-conservative and patriarchal movements within the Christian Churches traditional ritual practises, an emphasis on the sacramental mystery, vestments, and the 'bells and smells' of catholic and orthodox liturgy, an action which once again reveals it's unconscious alliance with liberal Protestantism. In doing so it has cut itself off from a space and set of practices in which its vision and theology is most easily realised and accessed.

The sacramental system is grounded in two notions neither of which is antithetical to the feminist vision. The first is that in Christ, time and eternity, the material and the spiritual, the divine and the human meet. Feminist theology often objects to the notion that this meeting took place in one historical individual and one particular time but this is to fail to take into account the fact that because time and eternity have met, there has never been a time when Christ was not. It is also to fail to take into account the fact that Christ's body is transposed into the multi-gendered, multi-ethical and multi-cultured body of the Church. We are Christ. The second notion is that the redemption, the liberation of the world is in process. Feminist theology was very quick to embrace process theology but with the notion of process comes the reality of 'not quite yet'. The night is far-gone, the day is at hand but what we stand in is the dawn, in a space of betweenness that contains elements of day and night. All is not what it should be. The sacramental system anticipates daylight often literally. Traditionally, the Eucharist has been celebrated by priest and people facing eastwards, towards the rising sun/son and traditionally the Eucharist was always celebrated in the morning, the time of the resurrection, the dawn of a new day, a new reality. The sacraments are the red pill of *The Matrix*, they literally incorporate participants into a new reality, the reality into a space beyond patriarchy, beyond the space of performance. Gordon Lathrop has argued that 'Christian liturgy orients its participants in the world'.[9] Liturgy provides the maps by which we interpret and navigate this world by taking us momentarily into a differ-

---

9. Gordon Lathrop ' "O Taste and See": The Geography of Liturgical Ethics', in E. Byron Anderson and Bruce T. Morrill (eds.), *Liturgy and the Moral Self: Humanity at Full Stretch Before God* (Collegeville, MN: Liturgical Press, 1998), p. 41.

ent world, a world that is subsisting and being brought to fulfilment in the world in which we move. This is the Background of Mary Daly's philosophy, the space of true Be-ing, where gyn-ergy exists in full realisation, a space 'over the moon'.[10] The mistake of feminist theology has been to concede to men and in particular those men who consciously invest in the most patriarchal mis-constructions of Christianity, the liturgical space because it is in that space in which the divine and the human co-operate in the work of redemption, the space of the magical, the space in which gender along with the rest of the material world is taken into the divine, transfigured and poured back out to warm and nurture the world with the first light of dawn.

In one of the most interesting works of sacramental theology ever produced, the theosophist C.W. Leadbeater argued that in the Eucharist humanity, divinity and non-human beings co-operate in the building of a Eucharistic 'form' which when completed is revealed to the clairvoyant eye to be a mighty cathedral-like structure, which is both the product of and receptacle of divine energy which at the end of the Eucharist is dispersed as 'a mighty shower of countless myriads of tiny snowflakes – not white only, but of every imaginable bright colour, which fall as gentle as *confetti*, spreading benediction wherever they go'.[11] This image is beautifully illustrated in the Blessed Sacrament Chapel in Buckfast Abbey, Devon, where a vibrant multi-coloured glass mosaic extends from behind the tabernacle to surround the congregation. For Leadbeater all the ritual elements of the Mass from the asperges, through to the use of incense and bells and vestments were necessary for the safe channelling of this almighty energy. Of course the primary channel is the priest. In Leadbeater's Liberal Catholic tradition the primary function of the priest is liturgical rather than ministerial. The priest is one who is set apart to act as a channel of God's grace. The notion that some may be set apart as channels of divine power in a liturgical context is not necessarily a patriarchal one, it only becomes such if the priesthood is constructed in such a way as the priest actually retains the divine energy and becomes the deposit of divinity rather than a channel of it. Interestingly, Leadbeater although locked into unhelpful gender dualisms in his own thinking, writing in 1920 he could foresee the possibility of women being ordained.[12] The ancient traditions of priestess-led rites, the female shaman,

---

10. Mary Daly, *Outercourse: The Be-dazzling Voyage* (San Francisco: HarperSanFrancisco, 1992).
11. C.W. Leadbeater, *The Science of the Sacraments* (Adyar: The Theosophical Publishing House, 1920), p. 289.
12. Leadbeater, *The Science of the Sacraments*, p. 391.

the wise woman, the medium etc., all suggest that women-centred cults recognised that some were set apart for sacerdotal purposes.

What is the nature of the divine energy that is channelled through the priest and explodes out into the world through the liturgy? It is the life of Christ, the reality that lies beyond yet underpins the constructions in which we live and move and have our being. It is the life into which we are incorporated by virtue of our baptism, a new creation freely given, not constructed, in which gender has no ultimate significance because along with our race, class and other socially constructed identities it is placed under 'eschatological erasure'.[13] This is not say that we are called to live beyond culture or its identity constructions, it would be impossible to do so. Christians must believe that the spirit moves through culture but it moves through culture transforming, transfiguring, destabilising, and allowing us no rest on our pilgrimage towards the divine. Gender and sexual identities serve many good purposes, they have themselves been important channels of grace but they have to be subverted because they are constructed in the context of power and are part of a matrix of dominance and exclusion. They grate against the sign of baptism.

Christianity has a divine mandate to be 'queer' to perform our socially constructed roles, our gender, our sexuality, our race, our class etc., in such a way to point to their non-ultimacy. It is the sacramental energy of the body of Christ in which embodiment is performed fundamentally different to the culture around that is poured out in the Eucharist and in the other sacraments. In particular, at the consecration of the elements the Church learns again and again of the instability, fluidity and transposable nature of the body as it recalls and re-members the body of Christ which was male but born of no male matter, transposed into bread and wine and into the multi-gendered body of the Church. It is in the Eucharist that the baptised learn about and anticipate the eschatological life. It is, as Cardinal Joseph Ratzinger has noted, a rehearsal of the life to come, a form of play in which we learn about and prepare for a life 'which St Augustine describes, by contrast with life in this world, as a fabric woven, no longer of exigency and needed, but of the freedom of generosity and gift'.[14] In the Eucharist then we step into the dawn, into the space between light and darkness, into the space between earth and heaven, into the incense that creates a curtain between two forms of life.

---

13. Malcolm Stuart Edwards, 'Christianity and the Subversion of Identity: Theology, Ethics and Gay Liberation' (PhD Thesis, Cambridge University, 1998), pp. 176-77.

14. Joseph Cardinal Ratzinger, *The Spirit of the Liturgy* (San Francisco: Ignatius Press, 2000), p. 14.

In the Eucharist gender has no ultimate significance, a reality that is conveyed in the vestments of the priest, the priest takes on a different form. Of course, confining the priesthood or any other liturgical function or office to one gender is a sign of contradiction and demonstrates a lack of understanding as to what is taking place in the Eucharist or what took place in the incarnation. Ironically, modern liturgical reform which has often led to the priest facing the people in a 'dialogue-Mass' actually draws attention to the gender of the priest in a manner in which the traditional eastward facing position does not. Rather than presenting the priest as a channel of divine energy which is poured out on all, it actually constructs the priest as the focus of the Mass rather than God. On the edge of heaven, gender differences, along with a host of other differences, dissolve and all that is left is our status as baptised persons. The mysterious energy that flows over us sends us to live out our culturally-negotiated identities differently, to parody them in order to better witness to the new creation being born in us. We live as people of a new reality, a reality that is mysteriously present to us in the liturgy and in particular in Eucharist. In the liturgy then, women enter into a magical realm, the space of between, the space of the dawn, the womb of creation, a space in which feminism reaches its fulfilment in the eschatological erasure of maleness and femaleness. It is the place in which queer theory conquers its own nihilism because here is its point and guarantee, participation in the divine life. It is a space in which the material orders are transfigured and become windows into a different type of living. It is the space of heaven of life beyond the power of death and life beyond the power of rationalism. In this space gender is dissolved, time is absorbed into eternity, miracles happen—bread and wine are transubstantiated, angels and the whole company of heaven including the dead are present with the living. In short, the liturgy, particularly the Eucharist, is a space beyond patriarchy although patriarchy has attempted to colonise it and feminism has largely retreated before it.

It is, however, vital that feminist theology reclaims the liturgical, the mysterious and the sacramental. First, for its own integrity it needs to practice encountering the mysterious, awful, Otherness of the divine. High liturgy simultaneously communicates both the Otherness and nearness of the divine and feminist theology needs to hold on to both these elements in order to avoid the patriarchal mistake of identifying the divine with a particular groups' experiences or aspirations. A sense of the disconnection between the divine and the human is essential if we are to be open to the prompting of the Spirit. Second, it is essential to keep Christian feminist theology rooted in the life of Christ which is re-membered in the sacraments and into which we are incorporated by virtue of our baptism. This is not simply the life of Jesus of Nazareth but our life too, it is the source of our be-ing, the wellspring of our energy, the rocket fuel of our praxis. Third, participation in the sacramental is essential for feminist theologians because here we encounter the magic with which we are to transform the world because we ourselves are transformed again into the living body of Christ. Here we are infused with a divine energy that enables us to live in the culture around us but in such a way as to transform it. Here we learn that all things are possible. Here we learn that patriarchy and all forms of injustice do not have the last word. Here is our Sabbath, our rest and immersion in the mystery of difference and sameness which inspires, refuels and propels us back out of the incense to struggle to bring heaven to earth, to make a perpetual Eucharist on earth, to not dissipate the mystery but rather to draw it down as our thealogical sisters do, to work its magic upon the world.

We who are feminist theologians must be careful not to follow our liberal Protestant colleagues in brushing side popular devotion or high liturgy as mere 'superstition', for our very hope and strength must come from a belief that small gestures can have huge significance, that it is possible for a new reality, a new energy to break into the world and renew it, that reality is thicker than its surface otherwise the point of protest, the keeping on keeping on, the chipping away at patriarchal structures and mindset will fade and exhaustion, arrogance and despair will prevail. But if we are conscious that 'angels and archangels and the whole company of heaven' are with us we cannot despair.

In the post-modern world the wall of dry rationalism has cracked and crumbled. Our sisters in thealogy have both contributed towards and taken advantage of this deconstruction in order to re-enchant the world and re-empower themselves. Christian feminist theologians must do the same if we are to sustain our struggle. We must step into the incense.

Sex and Death: Spirituality and Human Existence

Beverley Clack

Introduction: Human Being and the Spiritual Life

> The male soul assigns itself to God alone as the Father and Maker of the Universe and the Cause of all things. The female clings to all that is born and perishes; it stretches out its faculties like a hand to catch blindly at what comes its way, and gives the clasp of friendship to the world of created things with all its numberless changes and transmutations, instead of to the divine order, the immutable, the blessed, the thrice happy (Philo, *Special Laws* III).[1]

In this passage Philo, the first century Jewish philosopher, suggests the impossibility of basing a fulfilling spirituality upon the things of this world, which he explicitly identifies with the female. My intention in this paper is to explore the way in which this resistance to the world finds expression in the theories of humanity and spirituality that dominate western thinking. At the same time, I want to suggest precisely the kind of this-worldly spirituality that Philo rejects, grounding such an approach upon a feminist conceptualisation of what it is to be human.[2] Historically, the feminist engagement with the question of what constitutes human being and what defines the spiritual has been highly significant. Feminists have recognised the role that the normative status of the male has played in defining what it is to be a human being. Inevitably, conceptions of 'the human' have been based on male experience of the world: probably because those engaging in the process of definition (i.e., the philosophers and the theologians) have, on the whole, been male. In such a context, it is far from obvious what constitutes 'the human', and the work of foremothers such as Simone de Beauvoir has pointed out the importance of understanding the way in which patriarchal society has shaped our understanding of this concept. In her study of the way in which femininity has been socially constructed, she makes

---

1. Cited in G. Lloyd, *The Man of Reason* (London: Methuen, 1984), p. 25.
2. For a fuller development of this argument, see Beverley Clack, *Sex and Death: A Reappraisal of Human Mortality* (Cambridge: Polity Press, 2002).

her famous comment that 'one is not born, but rather becomes, a woman'.³ It is a comment that could equally be applied to the construction of human being. The traditional distancing of male experience from what might be called 'the life of the body' has influenced which features of life have been used to construct an account of what it is to be human. Thus the ability to reason, defined in contradistinction to basic physical existence, has dominated western theorising on the nature of human being, effectively distancing us from bodily experience.

Not only has the definition of human being been subject to the concerns of men: notions of spirituality have similarly been derived from male experience of the world. So, Janet Soskice has pointed out how difficult it is for women to pursue the spiritual life, for the dominant western formulations of isolated reflection are impractical for women engaged in the traditional female tasks of child-rearing and homemaking.⁴

In engaging with these issues, my intention is to ground a satisfying spirituality in the basic, irrefutable facts of our humanity. We are, at root, creatures who are born and who will die, creatures that reproduce through sexual relations. If we start from this position, what sense of the meaningful life can we develop? Shakespeare gives a graphic description of humanity stripped down to these essentials when he details the first meeting between King Lear and Edgar in his guise as the mad Tom. Lear sees in Tom a figure that stands for 'everyman', and points this out to his 'more sophisticated' companions:

> Is man no more than this? Consider him well. Thou ow'st the worm no silk, the beast no hide, the sheep no wool, the cat no perfume. Ha! Here's three on's are sophisticated; thou art the thing itself. Unaccommodated man is no more but such a poor, bare, forked animal as thou art (*King Lear* 3.4).

Rather than resist such conclusions, I want to base my account of the spiritual upon this idea of human being as a 'poor, bare, forked animal'. The western tradition has tended to resist such a view of human being, preferring, as we shall see, to focus on the experiences that might allow us to transcend such features. Yet, what if we accepted such a basic starting point? To what extent is it possible to ground a spiritually fulfilling life upon the basic facts of our humanity? In order to develop such a spirituality it is necessary to grapple with the concepts of transcendence and immanence that have been employed to shape human experience:

---

3. Simone de Beauvoir, *The Second Sex* (trans. H.M. Parshley; Harmondsworth: Penguin Books, 1972 [1949]).
4. J.M. Soskice, 'Love and Attention' in M. McGhee (ed.), *Philosophy, Religion and the Spiritual Life* (Cambridge: Royal Institute of Philosophy, 1992), pp. 59-72.

the main concern of this paper. In exploring these solutions to the question of our humanity, my intention is to move beyond such polarisations towards a more integrated account of human being and the spirituality that might be derived from it: a spirituality which takes seriously the fact that we are sexuate and mortal creatures.

Resisting Transcendental Accounts of the Spiritual

When talking of 'the spiritual', there is a tendency to understand this word as referring to a feature of human life distinct from ordinary physical existence. Commonly, the word demarcates a lifestyle based on a transcendent other, a lifestyle which distances us from the world in which we find ourselves. By starting from the premise that we are sexuate and mortal creatures, I want to suggest that we can think about the spiritual rather differently, seeing spirituality not as something which implies distance from the world but which is grounded in it. By reflecting on the sexual and the mortal we are able to derive a deeper understanding of the possibilities open to human beings.[5]

As such, I want to resist the idea that spirituality refers to a set of experiences distinguishable from ordinary human life. The ability to transcend our physical placing has categorised formulations of both the spiritual and the human, to such an extent that even diametrically opposed philosophies can be shown to accept this initial premise. Let us consider two such examples: Augustine's theology, and the existentialist philosophies of Sartre and de Beauvoir. A close reading of the work of these figures reveals the damaging consequences of accepting such notions for a positive evaluation of life in this world.

Augustine: Transcending the Sexual

For Augustine, the spiritual life is understood as that which transcends the physical, and most importantly, is understood in juxtaposition to the sexual. In order to be spiritual, I must give up the sexual life. Indeed, Augustine goes further than this, suggesting that if one resists sex, one opens up the possibility of conquering death itself.

Augustine's account of the relationship between spirituality and sexuality is based in his reading of the story of the Fall in Gen. 1–3. Augustine

---

5. It should be noted that I am not intending to deal explicitly with birth. It seems to me that the features derived from this category can also be found in the phenomenon of sexuality, which, after all, is ordinarily the means by which we enter into this world.

© The Continuum Publishing Group Ltd 2004.

uses this story to shape his understanding of the human condition. He argues that the story of Adam and Eve presents us with the vision of a humanity lost in sin. Sin is defined as the primeval act of disobedience instigated by the first human couple: an act which has ramifications for the very nature of human beings, for after this pivotal event, we are subject to the same laws as the animals who must reproduce through sexual intercourse and who are destined to die.

In this way, both sex and death cease to be understood as part of 'natural' human life, and are instead seen as 'unnatural', aberrations which arise from the Fall, and which bear the hallmarks of punishment for sin. Indeed, Augustine suggests that there is a direct and immediate punishment for this act of disobedience. Human beings are no longer able to control what Augustine calls the 'shameful' parts of the body: the sexual organs. Adam and Eve's disobedience is thus 'the origin of death in us, and we bear in our members, and in our vitiated nature, the striving of the flesh, or, indeed, its victory'.[6]

Augustine pays specific attention to the male orgasm, an experience that, he believes, reveals how easy it is to lose the image of God, located in the mind (cf. *On the Trinity*, Book XII). In the act of sexual intercourse, the god-like capacity to reason is lost: 'when he achieves his climax, the alertness and, so to speak, vigilance of a man's mind is almost entirely overwhelmed'.[7] In this sense, sex impacts not only upon one's ability to be spiritual, but also upon one's very humanity.

Sex is thus something dangerous, itself an intimation of death. Not surprisingly, therefore, it plays a particular role in the Augustinian construction of sin. Through sexual intercourse, the original sin of our primeval parents is passed on to each and every human being.[8] The womb is symbolised as the locus for death, and even the womb of Mary, the mother of Christ, is likened to a tomb from which Christ had to escape.[9] Sin is universal, and all stand in need of redemption. Only Christ, born of a Virgin Mother, is able to escape the universality of sin. In a shift that resonates with platonic philosophy, birth is associated with death, while death is seen as releasing us from this life.[10]

---

6. Augustine, *City of God* (trans. R.W. Dyson; Cambridge: Cambridge University Press, 1998), p. 555.
7. Augustine, *City of God*, p. 614.
8. Augustine, *City of God*, p. 573.
9. Kim Power, *Veiled Desire: Augustine's Writing on Women* (London: DLT, 1995), p. 180.
10. Plato, *The Symposium* (trans. W. Hamilton; Harmondsworth: Penguin Books, 1951), pp. 207-209; Plato, *Phaedo* (trans. D. Gaeley; Oxford: Oxford University Press, 1993), p. 64.

It is at this point that Augustine suggests a way out of this 'progression towards death'[11] for the one prepared to pursue the spiritual path. To live as God intends us to live, we must learn to control the unruliness of the flesh. Thus, Augustine's solution to the problems posed by the flesh is to sublimate human (sexual) desire into the (spiritual) desire for God. It is notable that he describes his relationship with God in overtly sexual terms: 'You [God] shone upon me; your radiance enveloped me; you put my blindness to flight. You shed your fragrance about me; I drew breath and now I gasp for your sweet odour. I tasted you, and now I hunger and thirst for you. You touched me, and I am inflamed with love of your peace'.[12] Yet this desire is immune from the vulnerability implicit in sexual relationships: the divine lover will never let us down; the divine lover is eternal.[13] Moreover, by moving sexual desire into the spiritual realm, Augustine sets up an opposition between the spiritual and the sexual. If one is to be spiritual, the sexual must be repressed: sublimated into the love of God. Of itself, sexuality is potentially destructive, and, as we have seen, it is the fruit of human sin. Sexual desire is thus linked with the curse of mortality.[14]

Controlling sexual desire for Augustine serves a broader purpose. Because sex is so linked with the curse of mortality, controlling sexual desire suggests the possibility of defeating death itself. Augustine appears to hold out the hope that sexuality might be controlled – 'our wish ought to be nothing less than the non-existence of these desires'[15] – that mind might subjugate body, and thus that we might be able to overcome the curse which fell upon humanity in the wake of the Fall. This is, however, something of a vain hope for Augustine: 'the accomplishment of such a wish [is] not possible in the body of this death'[16] and he tends to look forward to the next life where there will be no 'empty pleasure'.[17]

Augustine's reflections on sex tell us much about his attitude to this life. Value is understood to reside outside this world, and to be spiritual – to engage with that higher realm – one must affect an escape from the bonds of the flesh. This world might have been created by God (a

---

11. Augustine, *City of God*, p. 550.
12. Augustine, *Confessions* (trans. R.S. Pine-Coffin; Harmondsworth: Penguin Books, 1961).
13. Augustine, *De Sancta Uirginitate* (trans. P.G. Walsh; Oxford: Oxford University Press), p. 145.
14. Augustine, *On Marriage and Concupiscence,* in M. Dods (ed.), *The Works of Aurelius Augustine, Bishop of Hippo*, XII (Edinburgh: T & T Clark, 1874).
15. Augustine, *On Marriage*, p. 128.
16. Augustine, *On Marriage*, p. 128.
17. Augustine, *City of God*, p. 629.

comment that Augustine continually makes), but salvation ultimately lies outside it. While Augustine's focus is specifically upon the spiritual realm, the drive to avoid the conclusion that we are ultimately highly developed animals, whose meaning is grounded in the physical world, informs even explicitly anti-religious theorising. Self-consciously secular thinkers such as the existentialist philosophers Jean-Paul Sartre and Simone de Beauvoir have argued for an account of the meaningful life predicated on the phenomenon of human consciousness: thought comes to define the nature of human being. Despite their explicit rejection of the kind of Christian self that might be derived from Augustine's ideas, there is much common ground between the two positions. Just as Augustine suggests that the *imago Dei* is found in the mind, so Sartre's account of human being is based upon the contention that it is consciousness that defines us. Thus transcendence is similarly accepted as the paradigm for understanding humanity: a conclusion that renders the physical world problematic and dangerous.

Sartre and de Beauvoir: Transcending the Void

In developing his account of human consciousness, Sartre accepts Descartes' *cogito* ('I think therefore I am'). This statement, Sartre argues, expresses 'the absolute truth of consciousness becoming aware of itself'.[18] While there are significant differences — most notably consciousness for Sartre is always consciousness of the world[19] — Sartre accepts that consciousness has a transcendent quality: man is 'constantly outside of himself…it is by pursuing transcendent goals that he is able to exist'.[20]

This conclusion has a particular impact on the way in which sexuality is conceived. While de Beauvoir's theory of consciousness can be seen as a significant corrective to Sartre's,[21] both philosophers develop a fundamentally pessimistic account of sex as that which threatens to subsume the individual (invariably defined as male) in the physical (invariably defined as female). It is worth tracking this move in detail, for it reveals something of the continuing power of the paradigm of transcendence for

---

18. Jean-Paul Sartre, *Existentialism and Human Emotions* (trans. B. Frechtman and H.E. Barnes; New York: Castle, 1985 [1946]).
19. Jean-Paul Sartre, *Sketch for a Theory of the Emotions* (trans. P. Mairet; London: Routledge, 1999 [1971]).
20. Sartre, *Existentialism and Human Emotions*, p. 50.
21. Consciousness, she argues, 'like it or not' is embodied (see E. Fullbrook and K. Fullbrook, *Simone de Beauvoir: A Critical Introduction* [Cambridge: Polity Press, 1998], p. 60), and her work shows the — not always successful — attempt to balance the transcendent and immanent aspects of human life.

understanding what it is to be a human being, as well as something of the impact that this has upon understandings of woman's relationship with the natural world. For Sartre, the feminine stands for the world against which the individual must 'stand out'/exist. His account of the body builds upon this connection. While rejecting the soul/body dualism of the western tradition, in practice he maintains the inferiority of the body. The body might be 'a necessary characteristic of the for-itself',[22] but it is also 'there everywhere as the surpassed; it exists only in so far as I escape it by nihilating myself'. 'The body manifests my contingency'[23] and therefore if the 'I' is to attain the transcendence which comes through freedom, the body must be overcome.

From these comments it is not immediately clear that such a position demands that the body be explicitly equated with the feminine/femaleness. Yet consideration of Sartre's discussion of the qualities of slime and sliminess goes someway to supporting this connection. Early on he suggests a vague connection with women, writing of the quality of the 'sticky' as being akin to 'the flattening out of the full breasts of a woman who is lying on her back'.[24] If one pauses to reflect on this definition it appears rather odd. Visualise such an image and the word 'sticky' does not spring automatically to mind. It is only when the connection between the female and contingency is made that a clearer sense emerges of what Sartre has in mind when he uses this image. The female is 'a sweet, clinging, dependent threat to male freedom'.[25] She represents the world that seeks to subsume the individual in immanence.

The depiction of stickiness in *Being and Nothingness* develops into a discussion of the peculiarly *feminine* quality of slime: it yields, it offers 'a moist and feminine sucking', a quality with echoes of the abyss and death, for 'it draws me to it as the bottom of a precipice might draw me'.[26] In language that resonates with descriptions of decomposition, Sartre sees slime as 'the revenge of the In-itself'; it is 'a sickly-sweet, feminine revenge'.[27] Such language connects with Augustine's depiction of the

---

22. The 'for-itself' in Sartre's terminology is a being with the capacity for transcendence: the existentialist individual. The 'in-itself' in Sartrean terminology is immanent being—the world, physical existence. See, e.g., Jean-Paul Sartre, *Being and Nothingness* (trans. H.E. Barnes; London: Methuen, 1969 [1943]), p. 309.
23. Sartre, *Being and Nothingness*, p. 310.
24. Sartre, *Being and Nothingness*, p. 608.
25. M.L. Collins and C. Pierce, 'Holes and Slime: Sexism in Sartre's Psychoanalysis', in C.C. Gould and M.W. Wartofsky (eds.), *Women and Philosophy* (New York: Pedigree, 1980), p. 117.
26. Sartre, *Being and Nothingness*, p. 609.
27. Sartre, *Being and Nothingness*, p. 609.

sexual as that which pulls one into the abyss of natural life.[28] Sartre's humanism betrays a similar suspicion of sexual intimacy.

Yet, slime is not simply a reality that alludes to decomposition. It also resonates with the condition by which we enter the world in the first place: the sweat, blood, and mucus of birth. Birth *and* death are thus located in the feminine. In Sartre's novel *Nausea*, it is not the fear of death that causes the protagonist Roquentin such *angst*: it is the sheer gratuitousness of being which he finds sickening. And it is the female body that is linked explicitly with the appalling fecundity of nature:

> I toyed absent-mindedly with her sex under the bedclothes… I let my arm move along the woman's side and suddenly I saw a little garden with low, wide-spreading trees from which huge hairy leaves were hanging. Ants were running everywhere, centipedes and moths. There were some even more horrible animals: their bodies were made of slices of toast such as you put under roast pigeon; they were walking sideways with crab-like legs… Behind the cacti and the Barbary fig trees, the Velleda of the municipal park was pointing to her sex. 'This park smells of vomit', I shouted.[29]

Fertility is viewed with horror, and as the dream becomes more disturbing, the image of the woman pointing to her womb suggests that the horror of the female responsible for such life underpins it all. And this fecundity cannot be separated from death. The life that the female creates is destined for death, and the horror of the female organs as death-dealing as well as life-giving permeates the other memorable description of a woman in this novel:

> The cashier is at her counter. I know her well: she is red-haired like myself; she has some sort of stomach disease. She is rotting quietly under her skirts with a melancholy smile, like the smell of violets which is sometimes given off by decomposing bodies. I shudder from head to foot. It is…it is she who is waiting for me.[30]

We come from slime and we go to slime, and ultimately, despite the existentialist project of transcendence, no one can avoid such a destiny. In both birth and death the individual is ill-defined, dependent, dissolved, destroyed, and these are concepts which challenge the humanistic transcendental ethic offered by the existentialist. And such ideas are linked specifically with the 'problematic' nature of woman. As she is peculiarly responsible for birth, so woman becomes responsible for death, and thus in Sartre's transcendental ethic, woman is to be evaded,

---

28. Augustine, *Confessions*, p. 43.
29. Jean-Paul Sartre, *Nausea* (trans. R. Baldick; Harmondsworth: Penguin Books, 1965 [1938]), pp. 88-89.
30. Sartre, *Nausea*, p. 84.

just as Augustine's ethic, based on the hope of immortality, tends to distance itself from the body. The obsession with finding a life outside this physical world continues even in as self-consciously humanist an ethic as Sartre's existentialism, and it is worth noting with de Beauvoir that 'the values of Nature, [and] Fecundity' are of little interest to him.[31]

This desire to escape the immanent also manifests itself in de Beauvoir's feminist rendition of the existentialist project. Despite her attempt to bring together the transcendent and the immanent dimensions of our humanity, de Beauvoir's ultimate concern lies with offering *women* the possibility of a form of transcendence. While at pains to argue that the dualist rejection of the body is misguided, there is a tension in this account that becomes apparent with de Beauvoir's specific analysis of the female body. The body is peculiarly problematic for woman, as it is her body that has rendered woman 'the victim of the species'.[32] She has been defined as 'a womb, an ovary',[33] and is thus imprisoned in her sex in a way that the man's role in reproduction will not ensnare him. Indeed, the extent to which she is caught by the reproductive process is evident not only when she is 'creating' a new life;[34] menstruation is similarly problematic for it suggests that her body is 'an obscure, alien thing... Woman, like man, *is* her body; but her body is something other than herself'.[35] It has its own mysterious operations that continually convince woman that she is not in control of her destiny.

This theme is continued when de Beauvoir describes the qualities of male and female bodies. The male sex organ is 'simple and neat as a finger',[36] while 'the feminine sex organ is mysterious even to the woman herself, concealed, mucus, and humid, as it is; it bleeds each month, it is often sullied with body fluids, it has a secret and perilous life of its own'.[37] Nothing positive can be derived from such an organ, and one wonders what de Beauvoir would make of works that seek to establish the power, indeed wisdom, of the menstrual bleed.[38] The act of sex is also viewed as different for men and women, suggesting that the biological reality of being female differs fundamentally from being male:

---

31. Simone de Beauvoir, *Adieux: A Farewell to Sartre* (trans. P. O'Brian; Harmondsworth: Penguin Books, 1985 [1981]), p. 316.
32. de Beauvoir, *The Second Sex*, p. 52.
33. de Beauvoir, *The Second Sex*, p. 35.
34. de Beauvoir, as we shall see, disputes the authenticity of applying the word 'creation' to the 'natural' process of reproduction.
35. de Beauvoir, *The Second Sex*, p. 61.
36. de Beauvoir, *The Second Sex*, p. 406.
37. de Beauvoir, *The Second Sex*, p. 406.
38. P. Shuttle and P. Redgrove, *The Wise Wound* (London: Paladin, 1986).

> (M)an dives upon his prey like the eagle and the hawk; woman lies in wait like the carnivorous plant, the bog, in which insects and children are swallowed up.[39]

De Beauvoir even describes feminine sexual desire as 'the soft throbbing of a mollusc'.[40] Such language not only suggests a rather negative view of female embodiment; it also resonates with Sartre's descriptions of slime. Her discussions of birth maintain this negative perception. According to de Beauvoir, birth is not a truly creative act: 'she does not really make the body [of the child], it makes itself within her'.[41] Creative acts originate in liberty, and therefore the child is 'only a gratuitous cellular growth, a brute fact of nature as contingent on circumstances as death'.[42] In making such comments de Beauvoir implicitly accepts patriarchal accounts of what constitutes true creativity.[43] Moreover, it is 'not in giving life but in risking life that man is raised above the animal; that is why superiority has been accorded in humanity not to the sex that brings forth but to that which kills'.[44] Now, there may be a sense in which de Beauvoir is stating such claims with a view to critiquing them. However, nowhere does she give a positive role to the female as giver of life: hardly surprising, as the existentialist project is to 'stand out' from the world, not to be caught in its natural processes and cycles. De Beauvoir implicitly privileges transcendence over immanence, despite claims to the contrary.[45] Both of these qualities may be grounded in human experience of the world: but the female has come to be connected with immanence, the male with transcendence. While de Beauvoir is critical of the way the gendered account of these concepts has arisen, discounting such claims as 'vagaries of the mind',[46] she continues to privilege transcendence over immanence. Thus she writes with what seems a sense of horror that 'the feminine belly is the symbol of immanence, of depth'.[47] By way of contrast, the existentialist project is viewed thus:

> Every subject...achieves liberty only through a continual reaching out towards other liberties.[48]

---

39. de Beauvoir, *The Second Sex*, p. 407.
40. de Beauvoir, *The Second Sex*, p. 407.
41. de Beauvoir, *The Second Sex*, p. 513.
42. de Beauvoir, *The Second Sex*, p. 514.
43. See, e.g., Diotima's juxtaposition of physical procreation with spiritual creativity in Plato's *Symposium*.
44. de Beauvoir, *The Second Sex*, pp. 95-96.
45. Fullbrook and Fullbrook, *Simone de Beauvoir*, pp. 62-63.
46. de Beauvoir, *The Second Sex*, p. 44.
47. de Beauvoir, *The Second Sex*, p. 208.
48. de Beauvoir, *The Second Sex*, p. 28.

Similarly, for the subject to justify 'his' existence 'involves an undefined need to transcend himself [sic], to engage in freely chosen projects'.[49] It is at this point that liberation is a possibility for the female. Woman does not have to be subsumed in the processes of the body; she does have a choice. She, too, can become a transcendent.[50] The possibility of achieving transcendence becomes for de Beauvoir the feminist project, the hope that 'transcendence may prevail over immanence'.[51] The acceptance of a masculinist distancing from the world seems, then, to categorise de Beauvoir's thought. Her feminism merely asks that women be admitted to this process of distancing the self from the physical world.

Such are the continuing attractions and dangers of transcendent accounts of human being. Focusing on those aspects of our humanity that distinguish us from the rest of the physical world leads to a tendency to reject, or resist, basic human activities such as sex and birth. For Augustine, this rejection takes the form of seeking God; for de Beauvoir and Sartre, the emphasis is placed upon the pursuit of transcendence that enables us to stand out from the world. Such a project has considerable ramifications for women's lives: in order to become an individual, we must resist our connection with the cycles and processes of the physical world. But focusing our attention away from physical existence is not the only way in which a meaningful life might be established. And if we wish to claim that value can be found not in transcending the world but within its very structures, we will need to explore the possibility of immanental forms of spirituality. To engage with such insights is to take a step towards a more life-affirming account of the spiritual life.

An Immanental Spirituality

The dominant conceptions of humanity in the western tradition have tended to be based upon those features of life which suggest an ability to transcend one's physical placing. A distinction has been created between humanity and the rest of the physical world: a distinction that is expressed in both religious and secular thinking. In seeking a spirituality based upon an acceptance of the varied aspects of our humanity, and particularly an acceptance of physicality, such a model will not do. There is a tendency, as we have seen, for such transcendent models to reject the significance of the ordinary aspects of human existence, and to suggest

---

49. de Beauvoir, *The Second Sex*, p. 29.
50. de Beauvoir, *The Second Sex*, p. 82.
51. de Beauvoir, *The Second Sex*, p. 164.

that to some extent being human involves affecting an escape from the physical world. From a feminist perspective, this has been particularly damaging for women, who have been peculiarly related to the processes of reproduction. In order to balance such claims, it is worth considering the opposite possibility: that we might define both human being and spirituality by focusing on what might be called the immanent features of human existence. In other words, ordinary, physical, human existence might provide the starting point for our reflections. Perhaps the most significant theorist of such an approach was Sigmund Freud. According to Freud, the dominance of transcendence for conceiving human being was misconceived: rationality, the hallmark of being human for the philosophers, was largely illusory. More important and more powerful are the instinctual drives of animal existence, and the unconscious where such desires are repressed. A rather pessimistic account of human being is thus developed: we are 'sick animals', trapped between the heavenly realm of thought, and the reality of sex and death, unable to accept our fundamental animality, and thus destined to unhappiness.

Now, to accept Freud's model for human existence could lead to the conclusion that there can be no sense of depth or profundity. Yet this need not be so, as Freud himself suggests. A meaningful account of human life might be possible based *precisely* upon an acceptance of ordinary, mutable human existence. In the essay, 'On Transience',[52] Freud details a conversation with a young friend who was depressed by the transience of natural beauty.[53] How can we find meaning in a world which is constantly in the process of change, in which all that is around us is mutable and subject to decay? Freud disputes this pessimistic attitude to the natural world, noting that: 'a flower that blossoms only for a single night does not seem to us on that account less lovely'.[54] Jonathan Dollimore has suggested that this was a 'trite response'[55] to an overly earnest young man. But what if such reflections were taken seriously? Perhaps it might be possible to accept the reality of our animality whilst still finding meaning and beauty in life.

Freud's comment resonates with Martha Nussbaum's reflections on the possibility of developing alternative forms of transcendence. Nussbaum resists the idea that human being can only be defined in juxtaposition to the physical world. Just as Freud seems to suggest the possibility

---

52. Sigmund Freud, 'On Transience', in *Art and Literature* (Penguin Freud Library Vol. 14, 1990 [1916]), pp. 283-96.
53. Freud, 'On Transience', p. 287.
54. Freud, 'On Transience', p. 288.
55. Jonathan Dollimore, *Death, Desire and Loss in Western Culture* (Harmondsworth: Penguin Books, 1998), p. 181.

of locating meaning in an appreciation of the power and beauty of the physical processes and cycles of the natural world, so Nussbaum suggests that a form of transcendence might be grounded in the valuing of specific human experiences such as love and friendship. Nussbaum rejects the idea that it might be possible to construct one's values apart from the flux of human life.[56] We value most what is most vulnerable to change and chance. At the same time, she points out that we are not condemned to live 'as untutored biological instinct prompts',[57] but have the ability to reflect on our situation and act accordingly. It is the ability to reflect, grounded in the day-to-day experience of living, that Nussbaum defines as 'the transcendent'.

Such reflections suggest that we need not swing between the extremes of transcendence and immanence for understanding human being. Instead, transcendence itself might be grounded in the ordinary realm of human experience. We are now in a position to consider what such an account of human life might be like, and moreover, what kind of spirituality might be possible if such reflections are taken seriously.

Conclusion: Sex, Death and the Spiritual Life

At the beginning of this paper, we saw that Philo suggested the impossibility of basing a fulfilling spirituality upon the things of this world, identified with the female. It is precisely such an impossible spirituality that we have been moving towards in this paper. My contention is that a contemporary spirituality must be based upon an engagement with the basic facts of our experience. The reflections that follow are informed by the feminist concern to reject the dualistic construction of reality that dominates the discourse of the western philosophical and theological tradition. In such a context, human being has been defined according to those aspects that differentiate us from the rest of the animal world. The significance of Freud's psychoanalytic project is that he largely rejects this idea. Human beings are defined by the desires that stem from ordinary, physical existence. Martha Nussbaum's work suggests that it is possible to accept the conclusion that we are human animals, whilst resisting any claim that to do so is to render human life meaningless. She suggests a reformulation of the notion of transcendence that resists any dualistic construction. The transcendent is not that which overcomes the

---

56. Martha Nussbaum, *Love's Knowledge: Essays on Philosophy and Literature* (New York: Oxford University Press, 1990), Chapter 5.

57. Martha Nussbaum, *The Therapy of Desire: Theory and Practice in Hellenistic Ethics* (Princeton, NJ: Princeton University Press, 1994), p. 30.

© The Continuum Publishing Group Ltd 2004.

physical, but is rather grounded in that physical life. It is a term that embodies the possibility we have of reflecting on the experience of ordinary human existence.

It is this process of reflection which I take to be the fundamental ingredient of the spiritual life. To categorise the spiritual in this way does not mean that we neglect our physical placing. On the contrary: reflection is part of this human life. As Susan Griffin says, the mind itself is physical.[58] And to reflect on the basic features of our existence — sex and death — need not lead to an Augustinian rejection of the one in order to overcome the other. Rather, to reflect on these features can lead to a more fulfilling life, based upon the integration of reflection and relationship: possibilities that present themselves to us precisely because we are both sexual and mortal. Sex hints at the reality of intimacy, connection and relationship, while death suggests the need to engage with the experience of loss and loneliness that is also part of the human experience. Nussbaum is an Aristotelian, and, given this starting point, one of her central concerns is with the need for balance in our lives. In developing a contemporary spirituality, it is a useful model to adopt. We need to balance the reflective and physical parts of our selves. It is not enough to be subsumed in the sexual,[59] but neither is it enough to be 'brains on sticks', unaware of the desires which drive us, or indeed of the world around us. Balance is needed between what has traditionally been categorised as the transcendent and immanent aspects of our being.

It is perhaps this desire for balance that has led many feminists to focus on sexuality as the basis for a new spirituality.[60] Indeed, the neglect of this aspect of our humanity has had damaging consequences for the way in which notions of the spiritual have been formulated.[61] Yet, it is important that such reflections do not ignore the significance that death also has for defining our humanity. Death forces us to reflect upon the nature of our existence: how we are living, what it all means, what is important. Given that contemporary western culture effectively denies death's reality, it is vital that feminists engage with this feature, for to ignore death

---

58. Susan Griffin, 'Split culture', in M.H. MacKinnon and M. McIntyre (eds.), *Readings in Ecology and Feminist Theology* (Kansas City: Sheed & Ward, 1995 [1989]), pp. 25-35.

59. Reading the work of the Marquis de Sade who suggests precisely such a solution illustrates graphically the paucity of so living (cf. Clack, *Sex and Death*, pp. 80-103).

60. Lisa Isherwood and Elizabeth Stuart, *Introducing Body Theology* (Sheffield: Sheffield Academic Press, 1998).

61. U. Ranke-Heinemann, *Eunuchs for the Kingdom of Heaven* (Harmondsworth: Penguin Books, 1991).

© The Continuum Publishing Group Ltd 2004.

is to endow life with a permanence it does not have. At the very least, reflecting on death forces us to assess what we are doing, and to ignore 'the death factor' can easily lead to an overemphasis on the trivial rather than the profound. Contemporary western culture has distanced death to such an extent that it tends to be viewed as an accident that, if one adopts a suitably careful lifestyle, one might avoid. While the prevalence of an insurance culture may suggest that death's inevitability is recognised, in practice taking out an insurance policy can imply that this act offers protection against the transience of life. Death is objectified and placed in a category that makes it more manageable. In the process, it becomes something detached and distanced from my own existence. Ultimately, an illusion of control over death itself is constructed. My existence seems permanent, even necessary.

Similarly, western consumerism suggests that if I surround myself with desirable objects I will feel grounded in the world. The illusion of permanence derived from material objects is projected onto the self. The things I possess come not only to define who I am, but also to mask the fact that I am a mutable creature who will one day die. To resist such ideas it is imperative that we engage with death and the lessons that it might teach us. Reflecting on the inevitability of death necessitates that we consider how we are living: what is really important in our life? Moreover, it reveals something of the complexity of the life in which we find ourselves. Life involves the joy of birth, of love, of human relationship: features which all stem, in varying ways, from sexuality. But it also involves the sorrow of death, of loss, of rejection. There is a vulnerability associated with human life that must be addressed and incorporated into our reflections on what constitutes the spiritual life. To engage with this vulnerability is not to seek the kind of solutions that Augustine proposed. Shoring up the self in the face of death and looking to a world that is beyond such change and chance is not the only answer to the questions death poses. The engagement with death challenges the way in which we live: life is short and transient: what are we to do with it?

Reflection on sex reiterates that sense of the vulnerability and dependence of human existence. We are social animals, and what is most valuable about human life is located in that which is most vulnerable: our relationships with others. The meaningful life is not defined simply by the lonely attempt of the individual to find meaning, but involves creating and valuing human relationships. And of course these relationships are not defined only by loss: much joy comes from entering into loving relationships.

Indeed, the phenomenon of sexuality suggests that the human individual can never be understood in isolation from others. Relationship and connection are fundamental to the reality of being human. Sex also draws our attention to the fact that we are dependent not only upon others for our existence, but also upon the world itself. Love, which has an eternal quality in that it can survive even death, is grounded in the reality of human touching: kissing, caressing, even intercourse. Here in human flesh the eternal and the mutable, mind and matter, meet and merge. Taking seriously such fundamental features of human life makes possible a grounded spirituality. We are part of this world, and it is in the structures and cycles of this world that we can base the meaningful life.

With Critical Voices

Angie Pears

This occasion of a gathering of a group of educators and theologians who are involved in a variety of ways with issues of gender, theology, religious studies and sexuality coming together to celebrate the professorial inauguration of a leading scholar in the field offers a rare opportunity for critical reflection on the state of play of theology, religious studies and gender issues today. Such reflection is timely, and is significant in a number of ways. First, as a celebration of the academic standing of gender studies and feminism in religious studies and theology today, it recognises the widespread but not unproblematic impact that gender theory and feminisms have had on contemporary thinking. Second, given the rarity of a group of people engaged in a variety of ways with these areas actually having an opportunity to come together, it is an ideal forum for sharing and exploring different perspectives and interests. I would like to take recognition of the significance of this opportunity as my starting point to raise some questions about the challenges facing contemporary theological encounters with feminisms and about some of the challenges facing those of us who are engaged with feminisms and religion and Christian theology.

My own involvement with the study of Christian theology has come about through an interest and concern in the relationship between religion, particularly Christianity, and culture and society. I do not bring to this study any religious commitment or faith perspective as such but find the cultural and societal interchange with religion fascinating. I am especially interested in issues of gender and sexuality, as it seems to me that these are particularly striking and compelling examples of the problematic nature and tendencies of societal, cultural/religious interface. Gender and sexuality are both so central to human experience and existence, and yet despite this, or perhaps because of it, they both seem to cause Christianity and those involved with Christianity huge problems.

I became interested in feminist theological discourse because it seemed to me to be one way in which the relationship between Christianity and society could be unpacked and potentially, according to the claims of

Christian feminist theologians, if so desired, variously reconstructed. In this way, then, within the context of a critical exploration of Christian theologies I came to see feminism as a critical tool, and whether it is a tool of justice or investigation depends on perspective and motivation. My current research focuses on the strategies and methods of feminist Christian encounter and at a time when questions about the success and viability of feminisms are increasingly posed, it is an investigation into the methods and strategies underlying the often-creative relationship between feminisms and Christianity. It moves beyond questions of compatibility and incompatibility and identifies and explores key ways in which Christian feminist and womanist theologies are informed, sustained and made possible by feminist values and critiques. As part of this a number of important questions are emerging as significant, including, what is the state of play of feminisms today and in particular, what are the place and influences of feminisms in theology and theological education today? When questions like these are raised it becomes apparent that feminism seems increasingly to be perceived by some as irrelevant, past its sell by date or simply not effective as a tool of criticism and justice seeking.

There seems to be a radical dissatisfaction and rejection of feminism, and this comes in part from some of those who have been involved with feminism but who are now questioning its continuing validity and asking questions as to whether it was ever really effective. Susan Faludi, Camilla Paglia, Naomi Wolf and Rosalind Coward are important voices in the articulation of this dissatisfaction. For example, Rosalind Coward in *Sacred Cows: Is Feminism Relevant to the New Millennium?* claims that, 'Over the last few years… I found it increasingly difficult to say I was a feminist… I had become disenchanted with the idea of being "a feminist" in such times'.[1] With such concern over the current state of feminisms and feminist theologies there has been increasing talk in recent years of a post-feminism, and with it the announcement that we have moved beyond feminism, that we have in effect outgrown feminism. Whilst there is some lack of clarity about what postfeminism actually means and how the term is being used, clearly for some it has come to be seen as the end of feminisms. A different interpretation of post-feminism is that of Ann Brooks in *Postfeminisms: Feminism, Cultural Theory and Cultural Forms*. She argues that the term is a '…useful conceptual framework of reference'[2] for her, in effect, it represents '…feminism's "coming of

---

1. Rosalind Coward, *Sacred Cows: Is Feminism Relevant to the New Millennium* (London: HarperCollins, 1997), pp. 3-4.
2. Ann Brooks, *Postfeminisms: Feminism, Cultural Theory and Cultural Forms*, (London and New York: Routledge, 1997), p. 1.

age", its maturity into a confident body of theory and politics, representing pluralism and difference and reflecting on its position in relation to other philosophical and political movements similarly demanding change'.[3]

As well as questions being raised about postfeminism and the continuing relevance of feminisms there is also the extensively made claim that feminisms have in fact proved to be not only problematic but oppressive in their understanding, presuppositions and visions. A well-known but nevertheless vital problem with feminisms is what Mary McClintock Fulkerson has called 'the false universal in feminist appeals to women'.[4] In that some have contended that the same patterns of exclusion and marginalisation that have been identified in traditional theology have tainted the liberationist project of feminist theologies. Limitations have lead to claimed exclusions by those working from a diversity of perspectives including mujerista, womanist and lesbian perspectives.

There is an underlying issue for feminist theologies that has lead to a number of problems such as just detailed. Feminism has become normative and prescriptive, and tied up with a set vision rather than being visionary. Feminist theologies have been affected by the tendency to prescribe and solidify their position. This is seen, for example, in the feminist writings of Mary Daly. In her most important work *Beyond God the Father* there are clear indications that Daly is prescribing what amounts to a feminist ethical imperative for women to leave the Christian tradition. For Daly, there is quite simply no choice; feminist conscious women must leave Christianity in a move towards liberation. She speaks the language of revolution, conceptually juxtaposed to reformation[5], and the revolutionary nature of the women's movement means that the women's movement as 'exodus community'[6], moves beyond traditional religion. According to Daly, rejection is part of the process of awakening and throughout her writings she seems to have a very specific idea of what feminism rightly is and should be, and has shown herself to be highly critical and dismissive of developments in feminist theory.

Feminist values seem appropriate and important, and for many the development of a feminist worldview seems worthwhile, but the reality or the outworking of these seems to be that feminisms have become

3. Brooks, *Postfeminisms*, p. 1.
4. Mary McClintock Fulkerson, in Rebecca S. Chopp and S.G. Davaney (eds.), *Horizons in Feminist Theology: Identity, Tradition and Norms* (Philadelphia: Fortress Press, 1997), p. 99.
5. Mary Daly, *Beyond God the Father: Towards a Philosophy of Women's Liberation* (London: The Women's Press, 1986), p. 158.
6. Daly, *Beyond God the Father*, p. 157.

© The Continuum Publishing Group Ltd 2004.

homogenised and static. One of the most important ways for feminisms and feminist and womanist theologies to avoid such tendencies to closure and being prescriptive is to engage in open and critical dialogue. A self-reflexive feminism and accompanying critical questioning of feminisms is entirely appropriate and in fact essential. There is a problematic tendency among some of those who are engaged with feminisms and feminist and womanist theologies to argue that a healthy respect, which might well be read as healthy critical distance, should be maintained for early feminist voices. For example, the North American theologian, Emily Neill, in 1999 wrote of what she described as 'a disheartening trend among feminist scholars in religion and theology'[7] and is deeply critical of what she interprets as the progressive depiction of the development of feminist theological theory. Neill is concerned that the value given to the early writers of feminist theology is minimal, and that this is leading to a generational split among Christian feminist theologians. She envisages here a progressive understanding of new generation feminists which goes beyond, and in a sense diminishes the significance of, the work of the earlier Christian feminist theologians, what Marla Brettschneider has referred to as 'kill the mother syndrome'.[8]

It seems problematic to assert blanket approval of any set of ideas and remove them beyond the realms of critical exploration in hope of creative dialogue. Teresa Ebert in her feminist materialist critique of postmodernism, poststructuralism and feminist discourses, *Ludic Feminism and After: Postmodernism, Desire and Labor in Late Capitalism*, in exploring the issue of feminist criticism of feminism argues that:

> We thus need to ask why critique, when aimed at other feminists, is misrecognized as trashing, as uncourteous demolition. What is at stake in this misreading, and can critique be understood in more productive terms?[9]

Indeed, the radical implications of adopting a strategy of hermeneutic of suspicion, such as that detailed by Schüssler Fiorenza, is that nothing, not even feminisms, and perhaps particularly feminisms, stand apart from radical critical interrogation. At a time when questions are being asked of location and the future and critical edge of feminist theologies, such interrogation is crucial. The questioning of feminisms does not in itself necessarily lead to the rejection of feminisms, but the possibility

---

7. Emily Neill, 'Horizons in feminist theology or reinventing the wheel?', *Journal of Feminist Studies in Religion* 15 (1999), p. 102.
8. Marla Brettschneider, 'Horizons in Feminist Theology or Reinventing the Wheel?', *Journal of Feminist Studies in Religion* 15.1 (1999), p. 111.
9. Teresa Ebert, *Ludic Feminism and After: Postmodernism, Desire and Labor in Late Capitalism* (Ann Arbor: University of Michigan Press, 1996), p. 4.

that it might has to be accepted as part of the cost of a truly vibrant and critically aware feminist critique.

What is needed is a more critically fluid movement of feminisms and feminist and womanist theologies. Here, the changing faces of feminisms are important. Brooks has argued that postfeminism marks the moving of...feminist theory into a position which she sees as 'resisting closure of definition'.[10] Whilst recognising that the term may be problematic in some ways, it does seem that some of the ideas and intentions behind the designation 'postfeminism' are important and relevant. Going back to Brooks, for example, she argues that the 'paradigm shift' from feminism to postfeminism is seen in a number of different directions: first, in the challenges posed by postfeminism to feminism's epistemological foundationalism; second, in postfeminism's shift away from specific disciplinary boundaries; and third, in postfeminism's refusal to be limited by representation constraints.

Feminisms need to rediscover or re-establish their critical voices, and to constantly subvert themselves and this may well mean that what is left is not discernibly feminist according to what we have understood as feminist so far. In considering what all this might mean for explorations in theology and feminisms and how it might be imagined, the model of theological reflection proposed by Stephen Pattison in 'Some Straw for the Bricks'[11] as a critical conversation[12] is particularly useful. Pattison is attempting to break down understandings of theology as distant and removed and present it in an accessible and engaged way. He argues that theology can be approached as a three-way conversation:

> The basic idea here is that the student should imagine herself as being involved in a three way conversation between (a) her own ideas, beliefs, feelings, perceptions and assumptions; (b) the beliefs, assumptions and perceptions provided by the Christian tradition (including the Bible); and (c) the contemporary situation which is being examined... Each participant in the conversation will have questions to ask of the others...and each will need to get to know the others.[13]

Whilst the use of Pattison's ideas does not allow for direct translation into feminist theological contexts it does allow an approach to feminisms and Christian theologies avoiding the assertion of norms or prescribed

---

10. Brooks, *Postfeminisms*, p. 5.
11. Stephen Pattison, 'Some Straw for the Bricks: A Basic Introduction to Theological Reflection', in J. Woodward and S. Pattison (eds.), *The Blackwell Reader in Pastoral and Practical Theology* (Oxford: Basil Blackwell, 1999), pp. 135-45.
12. Pattison, 'Some Straw for the Bricks', p. 136.
13. Pattison, 'Some Straw for the Bricks', p. 139.

set ways. It sees encounter in terms of dialogue and conversation and at the same time allows for feminisms and indeed Christian theologies to be open to change, to be critically conversing rather than prescriptive.

In advocating such a model of theological reflection, Pattison argues that 'A real conversation is a living thing which evolves and changes'.[14] Such a model of understanding seen in relation to the encountering of feminisms and Christain theologies would allow for change, and to see the relationship as fluid. Any change of positions then would not be seen so much as a threat to the original visions or concerns of feminisms but as a necessary and inevitable part of the living encounter. Reflecting on those involved with this critical conversation Pattison argues that, 'The participants in a conversation are changed, both by what they learn and by the process of conversing with other participants'.[15] If we see feminisms, Christianity, and the individual or group involved with feminist Christain encounters as participants in a critical conversation, then we see that they must be open to change, because genuine dialogue or critical conversation involves the possibility of change.

Pattison's reflections on what sort of agreement is necessary for critical conversation are also important in the context of understanding how feminist Christian encounters might be understood and approached. Pattison argues that, 'The concept of conversation does not necessarily imply that participants end up agreeing at every point or that the identity of one overrides the character of the others'.[16] The history of feminist Christian encounters has demonstrated that the tendency to force agreement, to homogenise and overcome difference for the sake of apparent unity has proved destructive and oppressive. Some of those for whom feminisms and feminist and womanist theologies might be appropriate and effective critical tools of interrogation and reflection are concerned with the apparent lack of diversity and openness to possibility associated with these. And whilst the need to appear unified in the face of great criticism is understandable, it has not served feminisms and feminist theologies well. If the encountering of feminisms and Christian theologies is seen as an ongoing conversation that does not depend upon the agreement of all participants as either an indication of or step towards success, then the many different perspectives, experiences and needs of those involved might fuel the encounter with integrity and purpose. So that context and perspective, in their great diversity, are not a barrier to conversation but a determining and shaping part of it.

14. Pattison, 'Some Straw for the Bricks', p. 139.
15. Pattison, 'Some Straw for the Bricks', p. 139.
16. Pattison, 'Some Straw for the Bricks', p. 140.

© The Continuum Publishing Group Ltd 2004.

This is taken even further by Pattison with his understanding that not only do participants in a critical conversation not have to agree at all points, but that at times they may differ or stand back from the ongoing conversation. 'An important part of conversation may be that of silence, disagreement or lack of communication'.[17] So, again, this makes clear that resolution need not be the answer and closure, far from being the intended outcome, may in fact be problematic. The form of critical conversations such as that envisaged by Pattison is also important, for difference of form of engagement or at least the possibility of difference is important, '…conversation can be conducted at many different levels from that of preliminary acquaintance to that of long term dialogue'.[18] Some of the most compelling criticisms of feminism surround claims that it has not realised its goals. That the visions and aims of feminisms have not been achieved and so surely the effectiveness of such feminisms needs to be open to question. Perhaps the goals of feminism and feminism theologies need less surety and to be more open to change and not set up in a clear-cut linear way:

> As participants get to know each other, their views of each other and of relevant factors in relation to each other will change and evolve to become more complex and sophisticated. This does not, however, devalue the perceptions and insights gained on the first and perhaps naïve preliminary encounter, though later these may be radically modified and relativized.[19]

So, what might the implications of seeing feminisms in a more fluid and critically engaged way hold for understanding feminist and womanist theologies? First, such theologies need to regain their critical edge, rather than attempting to hold onto a precarious identity and space that often serves to alienate more that serve the needs of women seeking to use feminisms and feminist and womanist theologies as tools of critical engagement. As part of this critical explorations and the self-questioning of feminisms and feminist theologies are needed. Radical and possibly painful questioning of the insights, values and methods of feminisms and womanist and feminist theologies are needed. For those of us engaged with exploring the encounters of feminism and theology and religion there is a need to engage critically with each other on a challenging and productive level. It is possible to have detailed and creative conversation without either agreeing or without offending each other in disagreement. The implications of such engagement are important for the place of feminist and womanist theological engagement in higher

17. Pattison, 'Some Straw for the Bricks', p. 140.
18. Pattison, 'Some Straw for the Bricks', p. 140.
19. Pattison, 'Some Straw for the Bricks', p. 140.

© The Continuum Publishing Group Ltd 2004.

education institutions in Britain and Ireland. Clearly, there are different slants on the picture of the place of feminisms today but feminisms through gender studies and courses on feminist theologies and courses on religious studies and gender issues do seem to be holding a place of sorts in higher education institutions. Lisa's professorial appointment, and the appointment of others before her, gives recognition to the academic significance of the interface of gender, feminisms and theologies, but there is now a need for a critical forum for debate and engagement to move things on.

A lot of my own academic teaching and tutorial work involves working with Christian practitioners many of whom are bringing the critical insights of feminism into dialogue with their own context and theological reflection for the first time. Working in such an area, it seems that there is a huge gap in opportunities for detailed explorations and encountering between the theories and insights of feminism and specific contexts, and also between different interpretations and possibilities. If we take Pattison's ideas, it is okay to disagree, it is okay to start from different places and still be in conversation with each other and we do not need to be asserting one set of values to the exclusion of others. Critical dialogue is ongoing and creative and not predetermined.

On a personal level, I am entirely comfortable with feminisms not having the answers, such closure seems to limit and deny the very possibilities hinted at by the employment of feminisms as tools of critical insights. It seems more appropriate and fruitful to see feminisms as vehicles of exploration, as critical voices with fluid effect and movement. Such vehicles may break down, but this is not necessarily the end. I can change bits, overhaul it, put it back together or simply move on. This means that I need not be tied to either a set feminist agenda or a set understanding of what feminisms are, might be and might become.

BT
83.55
.E43
2004